MAX J. FRIEDLÄNDER
ON ART AND CONNOISSEURSHIP

1. HANS MEMLING
PORTRAIT OF A MAN IN AN ATTITUDE OF PRAYER
Lugano, Castle Rohoncz Collection

Hallward Library - Issue Receipt

Customer name: Holmes, Tom

Title: On art and connoisseurship / by Max J. Friedländer ; [translated from the author's manuscript by Ta
ID: 100019446X
Due: 19/03/2014 23:59

Total items: 1
22/01/2014 16:16

All items must be returned before the due date and time.
The loan period may be shortened if the item is requested.

WWW.nottingham.ac.uk/is

ON ART
AND CONNOISSEURSHIP

by

MAX J. FRIEDLÄNDER

With 40 Illustrations

BRUNO CASSIRER
OXFORD

TRANSLATED FROM THE AUTHOR'S MANUSCRIPT

by

TANCRED BORENIUS

First Edition 1942
Second Edition 1943
Third Edition 1944
Fourth Edition 1946

PRINTED IN GREAT BRITAIN BY ROBERT MACLEHOSE AND CO. LTD.
THE UNIVERSITY PRESS, GLASGOW
PUBLISHED BY BRUNO CASSIRER, PUBLISHERS, LTD.
31 PORTLAND ROAD, OXFORD

CONTENTS

CONTENTS

LIST OF ILLUSTRATIONS

ILLUSTRATIONS

8

INTRODUCTION

AMONG art historians of to-day there is hardly anyone who enjoys a position comparable to that of Dr. Max J. Friedländer. He is universally recognized as being probably the greatest living expert, notably, of course, on the early Netherlandish and German masters; and in normal times not a day passed on which pictures were not submitted to him for opinion from all parts of the world. But he is much more than the mere, if accomplished, expert, worried without respite by people eager for his verdict on their possessions: the list of his writings—all of them revealing the outlook of the born historian—makes a truly imposing series, culminating in his monumental *History of Early Netherlandish Painting* issued from 1924 onwards in fourteen substantial volumes. And for a long time the whole of this ceaseless activity had for its background Dr. Friedländer's connection with the Berlin Picture Gallery and Print Room: their marvellous growth during the period in question owes in fact an enormous debt to the distinguished scholar, whose career as an official came to an end in 1933, when Dr. Friedländer relinquished the post as Head of the great Picture Gallery, to which he had been appointed as Wilhelm von Bode's successor. It is, indeed, the very aroma of that institution in its best days which pervades the whole activity of one of the greatest of those who stand to it in the relation of at once alumnus and creator.

The opinions on art and connoisseurship, which represent the ultimate wisdom and considered judgment of a man whose performance has here been summarily outlined, must inevitably be of the most profound interest; and it is, indeed, a matter of congratulation that Dr. Friedländer should have made them accessible to a much larger audience than that of those friends in many lands who have been admitted to the privilege of his conversation. The views expressed in the present volume obviously derive a peculiar significance from the author's first-hand contact with the problems concerned, as well as from his power of independent thinking. In the Preface he characteristically stresses his lack of acquaintance with the existing literature on the theory of art, and readily, if over-modestly, admits the possibility that opinions similar to his 'may already have been expressed by others, perhaps even on the basis of better reasoning'. The students of aesthetics will, indeed, know how to value the judgments of the author precisely because they confirm the results independently arrived at by others. Thus—to give an example among many—when he speaks (p. 87) of a disinclination to use the expression 'beauty', it is interesting to recall the statement once made by Roger Fry: 'The word "beauty" I try very hard to avoid.'[1]

Very wisely, Dr. Friedländer has attempted nothing in the nature of a cut-and-dried system. In this connection it is worth while noting that his manuscript of the present volume is headed by the following quotation from Grillparzer:—'In these remarks I set out, regardless of any system, to write down, on each subject, that which seems to me to spring from its own nature. The resultant contradictions will eventually dispose of themselves automatically; or, inasmuch as they cannot be got rid of, are going to prove to me the impossibility of a system.'

The present volume is translated from the author's original complete manuscript in German.[2] The task of translation, if a thoroughly enjoyable one, has nevertheless presented considerable difficulties. The German literary vehicle, especially if handled by an accomplished stylist like Dr. Friedländer, tends towards a combination of characteristics—uniting boldness of exuberant construction to expressiveness—which is reminiscent of the Baroque; whilst the natural trend of English is towards the method of dissolving phrases into the simplest component parts, a method of which Basic English represents the most consistent application. I can only hope to have done some jus-

[1] See *The Burlington Magazine*, vol. xxxv (August 1919), p. 85.
[2] When last heard of, Dr. Friedländer was an émigré in Holland.

tice to the mastery of Dr. Friedländer's style. I have felt encouraged in my effort by the approval which he has been good enough to express of such occasional translations as I have made in the past of articles by him; and I particularly want to acknowledge the help which throughout my work I have received from Mr. Herbert Read, whose contribution towards the creation of an aesthetic terminology in English—notably in relation to German—has been of such importance. One or two brief passages in the manuscript, pointless in any other tongue but German—*e.g.* when relating to etymologies—have necessitated the very slightest editing.

In his Preface Dr. Friedländer has referred to the difficulty offered by the problem of illustrating the book. His own selection of illustrations has, of course, been incorporated with the present volume; but it has occurred to the translator that the author's meaning in certain cases might be made clearer by the inclusion of a few reproductions beyond those chosen by him. These additional illustrations are marked in the List of Illustrations with an asterisk.

TANCRED BORENIUS

University of London,
   University College,
      May, 1941

PREFACE

THE views set out in this volume are the outcome of personal experiences gathered during the lifetime of one man. It will help towards an understanding of the text, and further a friendly reception, if a few clues are given about the author, particularly about the manner in which he arrived at his general outlook.

Born in 1867 in Berlin, I grew up in a house which was barely two hundred yards from the Altes Museum. I studied art history in Munich, Leipzig and Florence, my natural inclination being from the start towards the attitude of the 'connoisseur' rather than that of the university lecturer. For the practice of the science of pictures I was fortunate in coming across three distinguished men as my teachers: during the time of my stay in Munich, Adolph Bayersdorfer; then for the period of a year—when I worked as attaché to the Cologne Museum—Ludwig Scheibler; and finally —when for decades I found myself a member of the staff of the Berlin Museums, the Picture Gallery and the Print Room—Wilhelm Bode.

Bayersdorfer, Keeper of the Alte Pinakothek, has written but little; without aiming at a far-reaching influence he, primarily by word of mouth, unselfishly shared his wide experience with others. His brochure *Der Holbein-Streit* (1872) and his posthumously published writings (Munich, 1902) give some idea, though by no means an adequate one, of the many-sidedness of his interests, the depth of his understanding of art, and that blending, which was characteristic of him, of acuteness, humour and the attitude of an eccentric, contemplative amateur.

Ludwig Scheibler shared with Bayersdorfer a lack of ambition, and like him has left a literary estate of but modest extent. Working untiringly, he grew into the first expert on the painting of the Cologne School, and on the early Netherlandish School. When in 1894 I was privileged to be taught by him at Bonn, his period of research was already a closed chapter in his life. At that time he was providing Carl Aldenhoven with facts, thereby making it possible for this litterateur with the schooling of a humanist to write his history of the Cologne School of Painting. Himself, he had by then turned to the history of keyboard music. The universal, tragic fate of the expert has been experienced by Scheibler with unwonted harshness. The many true things, which he had been the first to recognize and had expressed with pertinent brevity, became even in his lifetime common property; but his own name was mentioned almost only when it was a question of contradicting this or that 'attribution' of his.

PREFACE

Wilhelm Bode is survived by such fame as an expert, collector and organizer, and his importance for the blossoming forth of the Berlin Museums is still so dazzlingly present in everybody's mind that I need not devote many words to what I owe to him; to the stimulus and inspiration which his incomparable energy communicated to his assistant, who had the good fortune to collaborate with him during the decades in which the Berlin Museums were enriched in so truly happy a manner. Bode's fanatical eagerness for work, his universal connoisseurship and his authority, created a close network of connections with collectors and dealers all over the world, with the result that in his study works of art were offered for sale, placed on show and came up for judgment each and every day.

If I have failed to become an expert, the fault is, decidedly, to be laid at my door; it is impossible to ascribe it to unfavourable circumstances.

Inclination and official duty have led me to practical contact with concrete problems. When to-day, not without satisfaction and not without regrets, I look back upon the way in which, dissipating my energies, I have day by day with greater and lesser certainty given attributions out to the world, I feel the need of collecting myself, of explaining and justifying questionable activities.

In these essays I endeavour to reach an understanding in principle of the nature of art in general and painting in particular, I aim at a greater definiteness of terminology, and I build up for myself ideas as to the relation of scholarship to art. The first sections sound theoretical, with unwarranted intrusions into the domain of philosophy; those which follow deal with the practice of picture criticism. History of Art is touched upon in order to furnish proofs in support of my views, the instances being naturally chosen above all from the domain, familiar to me, of Netherlandish painting of the 15th and 16th centuries.

I am of the opinion that every true observation concerning any individual work of art may contribute to the better understanding of visual art as a whole, indeed of art activities in general.

Out of indolence, perhaps also from a sound instinct, I have hardly read any literature on the theory of art. It may be that most of that which has struck me, or occurred to me, has already been expressed by others, perhaps even on the basis of better reasoning. I venture however to speak from the conviction that knowledge, gained directly from one's own consideration of the work of art, as honest evidence possesses some educational value, and may claim some notice.

The illustration of this volume has been a troublesome matter to me. A reproduction is only justified if it supplements what is said in the letterpress, and if it makes understanding easier. I have been forced to recognize that over a wide extent of my studies the small monochrome reproductions are of no use. The

PREFACE

illustration has turned out meagre and unequal, only occasionally coming to the assistance of the written word with graphic force.

Certain things, here formulated, I have already before tried to express with different words, namely in the brochures *Der Kunstkenner* (1920) and *Echt und Unecht* (1929). I may perhaps hope that these observations and definitions, now worked into a wider context and submitted with better pleading, have gained in effectiveness.

To Dr. Grete Ring I owe a debt of gratitude for various helpful suggestions.

MAX J. FRIEDLÄNDER

I

SEEING, PERCEIVING, PLEASURABLE CONTEMPLATION

THE eye is, to the anatomist and physiologist, something like a *camera obscura*, a working arrangement of mirrors. What it means to see is, however, not explained, as long as we think of it as a passive attitude, as the mere reception of irritations by light. Seeing is not suffering something: it signifies doing something, it connotes spiritually emotional action. The word 'perceive' indicates that we grasp something with the pincers of the sense of sight and take something in.

At all events, here is an object from which light signals hit the eye. I know full well that philosophers deny the object, do not want to know anything about it; I side however with the empiricists and realists. If several painters at the same time, and under the same conditions of light, portray the same thing, pictures result which are different from one another; this has often been noticed and is a truism. Up to a point, however, the pictures resemble each other, and to the extent that they resemble each other, and inas-

much as they resemble each other, they afford evidence regarding the 'thing-in-itself'. The spiritual eye
works, setting things into order, supplementing, dis-
carding, selecting—not creating, not inventing. No
philosopher can forbid us to hold as true that which
we observe. If we do not believe in the object, then
we cannot explain how an understanding between
artist and spectator becomes possible.

I have a bunch of roses before me at a distance
of about two yards. The eye at rest receives the mirrored image of one of the roses, by no means of
the whole bunch. In order to take in the whole the
eye moves, and, in concentrating upon one part of
the whole, it cannot see any other, so that even in
this case of allegedly direct taking in of nature, a
visual action directed by the mind takes place, con-
sisting of a linking together of recollected images, a
gathering and assimilating of many impressions. Every
movement has its origin in the enquiring spirit. The
eye also moves while it accommodates itself to strata
of depth. Finally we see stereometrically with two
eyes. Seeing is hence not the taking in of a flat image,
but the combining of two images which give a twofold account of three-dimensional space.

We must differentiate as follows:

(A) The object, the fragment of nature, whence
    issue irritations by light.

(B) The image on the retina, on which, bit by bit,
    the three-dimensional object projects itself.

(C) The recollected image—which one might call vision—created by spiritually emotional action.

(D) The writing down, the realization of the vision by the means employed by the draughtsman or painter.

Already at the stage indicated by (B), more certainly when (C) has been reached, and not only when we arrive at (D), there co-operate habits which have formed themselves, possibilities of manual skill and intentions of reproduction—to which must be added knowledge of the object, which springs from previous visual experiences, and reports of other senses. The draughtsman's vision differs from that of the painter. Every artist arranges his inner sight not only in accordance with his own individual disposition, but also with reference to means of realization which are familiar to, and mastered by, him—means which, it is true, in their turn are dependent upon his individual disposition. The artist, says Nietzsche, paints 'ultimately solely that which pleases him; and that pleases him which he is capable of painting'. The draughtsman sees in nature drawings, the painter pictures.

It is not a question of that which is visible, but rather of that which we have perceived; and surprisingly little of that which is visible gets perceived, that is, absorbed into our memory of forms. Here is a crude instance. I have read a thick volume, and in doing so I have seen many thousand letters; if someone asked me in what type the book is printed, I note with amazement that I cannot answer this question.

The dividing line between working from nature and creating from imagination is generally too rigidly drawn. Strictly speaking, neither one thing nor the other exists. It is solely a question of differences of degree. When we draw or paint, we turn our glance away from nature, make an effort to realize a recollected image; and on the other hand the imagination in its free flights lives on the recollection of visual experience—it cannot give without having received. Keenness and vividness of the vision are much less dependent on the shorter or longer interval between the impression received from nature and the writing down, than on the intensity of the visual impression and the retentive strength of memory.

Hence you can well understand that Max Liebermann, a master who is labelled the consistent Naturalist, from his experience of creative work, extended the concept of imagination to his own productions; indeed, from his point of view he has with every right claimed that his imaginative activity is the only legitimate and permissible one. As a matter of fact every artistic activity which, in order to depict ideal forms, consciously frees itself from the memory of impressions from nature, runs the risk of falling into mannerism. Only an exceptional memory of forms enables the artist to fly away from earth. *Vestigia ter-*

rent. In the 19th century more than one artist whose visual imagination was not strong enough has got miserably stuck in thought, literature, non-sensuousness.

To the extent that seeing is a spiritual activity, the inchoate mass of colour dots gets sifted according to concepts. We interpret the dots which are communicated to us by the eye, and recognize a tree, a house, a mountain, an animal, the human body. To see is to recognize the outer world which is familiar to our consciousness.

Perceiving, we select that which attracts us, which pleases us, which is 'beautiful', as long as we contemplate pleasurably. We see differently, and different things, when we take notice with an end in view—say scent a danger—and our will gets worked up.

Schopenhauer knows no other happiness than the negative one of freedom from pain. By extending this thought to contemplation we can argue that the visible world is beautiful, is enjoyed, as long as it does not threaten us, is nothing but an image; as long as we may remain spectators before it. Not only the artist but everyone, more particularly the lover of art, stands happily gazing before nature, even if the non-artist only through art gets educated to such a manner of vision. The gap between enjoyment of nature and enjoyment of art gets closed, or at least narrowed down.

On the tombstone of each artist might fittingly be

written the words of Lynceus in the second part of
Goethe's *Faust*:

> *O happy eyes, never*
> *Unblest; for whate'er*
> *Ye have looked on, whenever*
> *It met ye, was fair.*

Thus speaks the artist born to see. Lynceus is, however, also the official guardian of the tower, and the
leaf is turned over, as he suddenly is reminded of his
duty:

> *Not for my enjoyment merely*
> *Am I stationed here so high,*
> *From the dark what horror drearly*
> *Breaks with menace on my eye.*

The glow of fire, the red flames are no longer 'fair'
to the guardian of the tower, because he is filled with
compassion for the old people, who 'will perish in the
smother' because his 'will' is summoned to consciousness of the danger, to action, to rescue; because
he is rudely awakened from the idleness of contemplation.

We are all of us both artists and tower-guardians,
to a greater or less degree, according as our soul reacts to the visible outer world. Life in a picture and
—practically the same thing—real life as a picture is
in a sense no business of ours; we have placed ourselves at a distance from it; its harshness no longer

2. MATTHIAS GRÜNEWALD, THE CRUCIFIXION

Colmar, Museum

Painted about 1510

hurts us; we have become neutral, unconcerned. We are grateful to the artist that he has carried us away from the evil world. Acting in life or suffering, we are creatures, chained to one another and ruled over; contemplating, we feel ourselves as lords and masters. It is impossible, to be sure, wholly to discard elemental feelings, such as sympathy with sorrow or joy, care and fear; but communicated to us through a work of art they alter their constituent qualities. The aestheticians generally declare that this alteration is due to a re-shaping, stylizing purification and that the secret of artistic effect is herein contained. This is an explanation which, whether true or false, has had a deplorable effect on the creative artists who, thus enlightened, have wilfully taken to emasculating life, with questionable results.

Let us think of Grünewald's *Crucified Christ*, which displays the maximum of bodily suffering crudely, closely, over-distinctly. Why is the aspect of this bearable? Why does it not release a torrent of horror, which sweeps away all pleasurable contemplation? Because, in spite of the utmost closeness to nature, not the tortured body but the picture of it rises before us; because the master communicates to us his vision and, thereby, his religious fervour in such purity and so decisively, that our imagination, removed far away from disturbing, unrelenting actuality, experiences the distant, sublime myth; and the fearsomeness becomes deeply affecting drama. In the picture Christ dies not once, not here: on the contrary, everywhere and always; hence never and nowhere.

In the extreme case which the boldness of Grünewald's genius offers us, much is demanded from our willingness, our readiness to meet half-way; and time passed before Grünewald had educated lovers of art, had made them ripe for his vision—and he has perhaps not even yet succeeded in the case of everyone.

In every instance the fragment of nature which appears in the work of art has, not without loss or gain, been filtered through the nature of one man, existing individually and for once. We perceive what the artist has seen—as far as we are able to do so.

Enjoyment of art and of nature are mingled; and an attempt at analysis produces complicated results.

I contemplate, say, a landscape picture by Cézanne, and can understand it because I have perceived similar motifs in nature. Nature is lasting, eternal; the changing styles are ephemeral: thanks to our experiences of reality we can more or less reach an understanding with artists of all periods. I go into the open air, after having looked at a picture by Cézanne, and perceive in nature paintings by Cézanne. I have learnt to see from the master. This one finds often formulated thus or similarly. Now I cannot, however, see more than my disposition permits, and scarcely what Cézanne has perceived. Moreover the work of art is a fragment of nature seen through a tempera-

3. PAUL CÉZANNE, AUVERS-SUR-OISE
about 1885

ment, but I see the picture by Cézanne through my temperament.

All things considered it is impossible to deduce more than this: the lover of art perceives nature as well as art with his own eyes, the same eyes, only that artists have given direction to the way of seeing. The lover of art learns from nature to understand works of art, from works of art to enjoy nature.

The 'disinterested pleasurableness' of which the aestheticians are so fond of speaking, is not to be taken too literally. If I sit in the auditorium I am, it is true, not taking part in the events on the stage, but I am not unconcerned. My curiosity and my thirst for knowledge get stimulated. 'Disinterested' can here only mean that the events in question do not belong to the reality to which I am harnessed; I am able to look at them as it were with the blissful eyes of the deceased. A *genre* picture reminds me of domestic happiness, of homely cosiness, or of gay parties—of conditions and experiences of my own reality. Landscape pictures call up memories of travels and excursions, of parts in which I have loved to stay or else have experienced something tragic. But everything is transfigured and lightened, bereft of its sting, as it were at a distance of time and space. Voluntarily, without being constrained, I turn to the portrayal— this is a decisive point—and in so doing gain the superior restfulness, the happiness of pure contemplation. Art creates a second world, in which I am not an actor but a spectator, and that world resembles Paradise.

Art performs the function of a servant in that it adorns, reports, tells a story, teaches, embodies ideals, awakens devotion. Under the protection of the Church, art has expanded brilliantly. Artists shook the barriers of pure visual art and could with impunity take up with myth, poetry, satire and anecdote, as long as they communicated intellectual or spiritual values exclusively by means of form and colour.

Roughly and generally speaking, a development in the direction of absolute visual art may be traced in history. The motto *l'art pour l'art*—'art for art's sake'—which gained currency in the 19th century, proclaimed a desired end. One arrived at emancipation, as once from the Church, so now from poetry, mythology, history; and threw oneself into the arms of visible nature.

The suppression of human sympathy has now and then been evinced most emphatically by the French Impressionists. Thus Monet once said to Clemenceau: 'I am standing by the bed of a dead person, a woman whom—well, I had loved very much indeed . . . and still loved very much. I looked at her eyelids. I said to myself: "There is a kind of purple . . . what kind of blue is contained in it? And red? And yellow?"' The absolute visual art was preparing to become inhuman.

The Impressionists have made it a plank in their programme to eliminate everything that stands for spiritual orderliness and interpretation in favour of appearance to the senses: with them it becomes true in real earnest—'Whate'er ye have looked on, whenever it met ye, was fair'. Subjectively speaking, in their emotional attitude towards the visible world they succeeded in carrying out this part of their programme; but not objectively speaking, so far as the result is concerned. Their eye is an organ in the spiritually emotional whole, whose inclinations and interests decide the choice of the standpoint, the direction of the glance, the object. Hence their works are no less stamped with personality than those of the intentionally idealizing painters.

A last consequence has been drawn by what is known as abstract art. Even now it seemed that out of nature too much spiritualness, too much thought, streamed into the picture. Following up the endeavour after visual art, one turned one's back on Nature.

The irony of this last change of front—or is it the last but one?—lies in this, that those who were bold and radical ended up in the primitive category, ornament—an ornament that fulfils no serving function but hovers in empty space, free as a bird.

That which prevents us from speaking of pure visual art in front of a picture or a sculpture, lapses completely in front of ornament, which is mere decoration. Here there mingles into the play of form and colour values nothing of associated ideas or any reminiscence of our reality. If we try roughly to

29

differentiate from one another the concepts of Emotion and Feeling by calling the stirring and irritation of the soul emotion, and the stirring of the senses feeling, then we may say that ornament appeals more to feeling than to emotion. The play of mastered forces satisfies the need of entertaining the sense of sight, and through symmetry, and the turn and return of the identical feature, symbolizes order and the rule of laws: it arouses general spiritual moods such as rapture, tension, gaiety, lightness, balance or restlessness.

It is half praise, half blame when you call a work of art decorative. A Persian carpet, a piece of brocade cannot, will not, and ought not to be anything more than decorative. If however I call a picture 'decorative', then this verdict contains a derogatory note, since by recognizing a satisfying stimulation of our senses a lack of more profound effect is admitted. Now since every more profound effect touches upon matters of spirit and thought, upon human destiny, it follows that Art free and noble is less pure visual art than the art which serves and adorns; than industrial art.

Architecture has, subtly and somewhat wrong-headedly, been called frozen music. For architecture, tied to a purpose and serving needs, stands in contrast to music. More properly you might call ornament visible music, and music audible ornament, only that music affects the life of our soul more profoundly than does ornament.

I have spoken of 'seeing', but in so doing I have

come to the chapter of creation—quite naturally, since the reader no doubt will have noticed that the activity of the formative artist is essentially contained already in the action of seeing, not only in execution, in concretizing that which has been seen.

To make, to shape, to carry out, to produce, to execute, to draw, to create: all these are words which are used about the genesis of a work of art. The French have a particularly pregnant word, *réaliser*, which means 'to transform vision into something which we can apprehend with our senses'. 'To make' is a colourless, neutral expression, indicating an action whose result stands before us in the work of art. 'To shape' indicates an action conscious of its aim. 'To carry out', 'to produce' hint at an obscure region, where the artistic form remains hidden until the artist has brought it out into the light. 'To draw', thus to get something out of water, pre-supposes an existing matter, a chaos out of which the work of art is taken. You 'execute' a copy or a replica; and the sober word indicates that the work of art was pre-existent to the performance. The nearer we get to the concept of genius, the more appropriate are verbal images of such mystical sublimeness as 'create', though strictly speaking there is no originating out of nothing. The expression 'to invent'—from the Latin *invenire*, to find—really contains a legitimate doubt as to independence of creation, since a 'find' obviously must have had a previous existence.

II

EXISTENCE, APPEARANCE, OBJECTIVE INTEREST IN THINGS

THAT which exists is given to the eye as appearance. The spirit interprets appearance, and deduces from it something that exists, builds up its vision and thereby the work of art; in so doing it not only supplements, fills in and emphasizes, but also exercises tolerance, forbearance and selection.

The relationship of the artist to the appearance, existing here and now, will be modified in accordance with his conception of his task, of that which he has to create and wishes to create. The countless degrees may roughly be classified in three categories, chronologically following upon one another.

As long as the master had to depict divinities or saints, to retell legends or myths, he took as his starting point spiritual conceptions and emotions of the soul—if not a pictorial tradition—and used impressions from nature in order to invest his creations with the illusion of being alive and having the possibility of existence.

In order to cope with his task, he did not have the

least occasion to observe a feature of nature in its accidental setting and context, or even to regard it as picture-worthy. He 'took', he singled out and picked out, that which he required for his purposes. Gottfried Keller speaks somewhere of 'the sneaking thefts of the artist'. How little did a Greek vase-painter, or a medieval painter of altarpieces, need! Little, not indeed from incompetence, from lack of accurate vision—the little is not infrequently astonishingly true to nature—but, on the contrary, because the immensely much—and notably earthly space and individual character—not only did not serve his intentions, but even threatened to degrade, to confuse and to defile his vision and thereby his work. He had to show something which, as a whole, was not to be seen in the open air, and took as his starting point a pictorial idea, not a visual experience.

Every period asks for naturalness in a different degree. That which centuries ago seemed natural impresses us now as stylized.

The period of myth, faith and superstition was succeeded by a period full of curiosity, the period of discoveries. Interest turned from the invisible Creator to visible creation. With the 15th century the artist becomes something like a devotee of natural science. His observation gains in neutrality, tolerance, and many-sidedness. More especially, increasing attention was given to the organic connection of things such as that of man and space and light. That which exists is no longer rendered according to preconceived ideas, but in conformity with appearance: and appearance was trusted to the extent that it promised to give reliable information about the gay and confused world, which now had become picture-worthy. Anyway, visual experiences were combined and arranged with the intention of displaying reality in a lucid view.

An objective interest in things—born of thirst for knowledge—intervened in this tendency. We expect to find such an objective interest, in its purest form and its highest degree, in a dry-as-dust botanist, who examines the leaf of a tree. To start with, the botanist knows more about the leaf than the artist does, and hence he sees more. Upon his observation there is, however, imposed a limit, because the leaf interests him not as an individual but as a specimen of its species. That every leaf of a tree differs from every other leaf of the same tree is something which can only disturb or confuse the botanist. It is also a source of trouble to him, that the object of his scholarly attention, in its location in space, in its distance from the eye, in the given conditions of light, appears disfigured, bent, foreshortened and discoloured. What concerns him is the inherent shape and colour, freed from everything accidental, of the leaf.

A purely objective interest in things is, indeed, a stranger to art, but in conjunction with formative power it is capable of fecundating artistic production.

Thus Dutch painting in the 17th century has profited freely enough from the thirst for knowledge in relation to that which exists—a fact which becomes particularly patent in the work of artists of more modest talent and lacking in imagination. If the vaunted Dutch 'Realism' failed to grasp individuality in the degree that might have been expected, this is to be explained as follows: A report on existing matters, accurate and dependable as a record, was asked for and produced; but one was not permitted to content oneself with appearance—this had to be supplemented from knowledge, which brought about an approach to type. An exception, of course, is supplied by portraiture, in the case of which the objective interest in things and response to individuality overlap.

The Dutch painters were specialized experts on real things. Potter knew cattle like a farmer, Saenredam buildings like an architect, Willem van de Velde knew all about shipbuilding.

Just as the objective interest in things, so did the tendency towards narration invade painting. Jan Steen was not impunely a witty judge of men and an inventive writer of comedies. As regards native talent not inferior to any contemporary or fellow-countryman, he did not as a painter achieve, or at least did not retain, the uniform mastery of a painter like Gerard Terborch, to whom discretion taught the wisdom of restricting himself. All too loud and all too pointed when he tells a story, makes merry or entertains, Steen often sacrificed the conscientiousness of execution. Intellectually active painters ran the risk of crossing the boundary where the visible world comes to an end and the imagined one begins. The harm which the inclination to be 'poetic' did to art in the first half of the 19th century is obvious.

In the second half of the 19th century painters turned their backs on poetry, history and anecdote. As the objective interest in things waned, and the tendency towards narration was suppressed, art became independent and autonomous. The relationship of the painter to appearance altered once more. The philosophers have thrown suspicion on 'the thing-in-itself', and have declared appearance to be a creation of the human spirit. From sound instinct—if not in defence of legitimate interests—the artist is bound to oppose this view. Nevertheless, in the 19th century there arose everywhere—as a positive deduction from that negative doctrine—an enthusiastic regard for appearance. If the philosopher said pessimistically 'Reality is nothing but appearance', the artist replied optimistically 'Appearance is reality'. From fear of destroying the organic connection, the painters came to look upon composing, stylizing, supplementing, in brief upon every active intervention, as bungling. Impressionism directs the artist to a standpoint from which he, without misgivings, must portray that which enters his field of vision. Confidence in the unique visual experience entails heightened illusion;

accidental singling out of the scene; broad, quick handling of the brush; indifference to inherent form and inherent colour: since all things appear as accidentally conditioned by their location in three-dimensional space, and given circumstances of light. Since one no longer takes concepts as one's starting point, type gives way to individual form. The painter lets the picture report, excite, tell a story—'lets' in the sense of *laisser*, not of *faire*. He is reluctant to become an interlocutor.

Jan van Eyck, when he painted a brocade mantle, subordinated himself, with an objective interest in things, to an existing object: and he created something that produces the same impression as a real brocade mantle, whereas a Manet contents himself with the appearance. It is not to be objected, that this difference only consists in a subjective notion: it is patent enough in the result. Jan van Eyck's work is productive of illusion if we stand at a distance of one foot, three feet or two yards, whereas the work of Manet is tied in its effect to a definite point of vision— the very one from which the painter has given his rendering of the object.

Van Eyck's eye moved in front of a world at rest; Manet's eye rested in front of a world in motion.

I want to avoid the impression of my labouring under the delusion of being able to assign to each master a room on one of the floors of a mansion. Every painter—entirely apart from the period to

37

which he belongs—according to his individual disposition takes up a different attitude towards appearance from that of every other. Especially from the 15th century onwards boundaries have been displaced. Masters of genius—such as Titian or Rembrandt towards the end of their careers—surmount the barriers which I have set up. Richness and complexity of production refuse to be compressed within a formula.

Anyway there remains recognizable one essential, main tendency: the transition from active, selective fashioning to receptiveness, to unreserved and reverent devotion to the many-coloured reflection of life, and unquestioning acceptance of that which is given us precisely here and now in a connected fashion.

III

ART AND SYMBOL

COMMON to all artistic activity directed towards imagery is the task of making something that has been seen by the spiritual eye accessible, through this or that manual procedure, to the physical eye. That which has been seen is a complex of that which has been taken in by the senses and put into order by the spirit. The relation of these two factors to one another determines the countless manners of art, differing from each other, which have emerged in the course of historic evolution.

The aestheticians interpret the secret of art, taking Plato as their starting point, by considering that the thing to be reproduced is not the appearance, offered here and once, but rather the idea—thus an image which exists in imagination as the deposit of many visual experiences, which is perfect, beautiful, cleansed of everything accidental. However dangerous this theory may become to the creative artist, and questionable as a norm for the judge of art—but fortunately the relations between aesthetics and artistic judgment are extremely slight—it is possible by subtle interpretation to give it something like universal validity.

If we remember that even a consistently naturalistic painter, who portrays a rose which stands before him, has seen many roses, recognizes the rose *qua* flower, that he perceives of the motif only what pleases him and what he expects to see, then we approach the theory of Plato and are able to say with some justification that the 'idea' of the rose is the thing to be portrayed. This theory, however, only holds good if, in relation to a given stage of art history, it is restricted or expanded, since the individual visual experience and hence the individual appearance in the course of historical evolution has determined artistic form with increasing strength. From a non-philosophical standpoint we prefer instead of an 'idea' to speak of a 'clarified recollected picture' which differs from the individual item through its value as a symbol.

The symbol is a sign which, through convention, habit or immediately through its form and colour awakens notions which it is incapable of conveying explicitly. In the symbol the visible represents something invisible, as the letter represents the sound. The banner signifies home, country and patriotism. All art is symbolic, since the artist through image, word or note communicates to the spectator or listener by the material the transcendental, by the sign the thought or emotion, by the particular the general, by the example the category.

In front of a Greek statue, no one can mistake the symbolizing function of art. The beautiful youth represents the God. Art, inspired by religion, is obviously symbolic, presenting as it does things human and of the earth as superhuman. The halo is a palpable symbol. And even if, in the course of artistic evolution, the symbolic effect seems to conceal itself, it never disappears. By the capacity to overcome the narrowness of the individual case, the formative power may be recognized; and by the ease with which that which is visible or audible points beyond itself, the artistic value may be measured. We must, however, pre-suppose that artist and spectator understand each other, that the artist is strong enough to raise the spectator to his own level, and that the spectator is ready to allow himself to be so raised.

Architecture and music awaken general impulses or vibrations of the soul; sculpture and painting rather more particular ones, and such as have been modified by thought.

Symbol is not to be confused with allegory. The former addresses itself partly to the senses, partly to the emotions; the latter—as a riddle or a charade— to the intellect, and is, from its essence, a questionable vehicle of art.

All art is bilingual, speaks as well as sings. In showing something factual, concrete, it communicates at the same time spiritual feelings. Only, the listener or the spectator must be capable of reception. Otherwise it might happen, that someone might read a line like Goethe's *Ueber allen Gipfeln ist Ruh* as if it were a weather report. The formative artist offers signs which on the one hand enable us to recognize something of the familiar world around us, on the other convey to the spectator the artist's conception of it, his judgment on it and the pleasure he derives from it.

Often and not without reason have art and play been brought into connection with one another. Especially when the earliest expressions of artistic activity are analysed, and the ever burning question of the origins of art is being ventilated, do we come upon results akin to those which we arrive at when investigating the play of children. The child plays, and so does the domestic animal—the child who has not yet been claimed by the struggle for life, the animal which is no longer claimed by it. To play is nothing but the imitative substitution of a pleasurable, super-fluous and voluntary action for a serious, necessary, imperative and difficult one. At the cradle of play as well as of artistic activity there stood leisure, tedium entailed by increased spiritual mobility, a *horror vacui*, the need of letting forms no longer imprisoned move freely, of filling empty time with sequences of notes, empty space with sequences of form.

IV

FORM, COLOUR, TONALITY, LIGHT, GOLD

FORM and colour are tied to one another. There only exists coloured form, and—which is the same thing—colour that has been formed. Everything visible consists of parts, which are forms, colours or notes, according to the quality which one takes under consideration. The extent, quantity and boundary of the part is called form; its content and quality is called colour; its degree of light, tonality. The limit of form lies where one colour ends and another begins. The human mind has divided up the unified appearance. It is true that the selecting, isolating, even partially blind visual action is able to disregard colour or at any rate to neutralize it, but even in an extreme case such as that of the outline drawing, black and white—which after all are also colours— remain indispensable for the sake of visibility. Conversely, the boundary of the part called colour may have become indistinct or obliterated, in which case report and information as regards that which exists lose in clearness. Form addresses itself more to understanding, colour rather to feeling. Colour produces an immediate effect as a symbol. White suggests that which is empty, immaculate, innocent. Form and colour stand in the same relation to each other as word and note in a song. On the effect of the various colours on the mind, on the mood, Goethe has spoken in great detail in his *Theory of Colour*. It is strange, by the way, how his sense of colour, so amazingly sensitive in front of nature, is of so little avail in his judgment of art.

We come upon the contrast between pictorial method of vision, and the draughtsman's method of vision. After I have seen a red circle I can retain in my memory the circular outline or the red colour, according as to whether I am rationally or sensually minded or disposed.

God did not first create the world, and then proceed to paint it. The dividing up of appearance was furthered by the educational curriculum, the method of work and academic teaching. One dealt with that which is visible in conformity with the advice: *Divide et impera*. One drew *and* one painted. As students attended to these activities, isolated from one another, their visual memory lost the organic connection between form and colour, and they often added to form an unsuitable colour. Their attitude towards form was earnest, conscientious and reverent; towards colour arbitrary and playful.

The 15th century painter will, say, introduce into his composition the figure of a saint which, four or five inches high upon the picture surface, seems to stand at a considerable distance from the eye of the spectator; his red robe shows however an intensity of tonality which corresponds to a far smaller distance. Form and colour are here not seized with the same visual grasp, nor from the same standpoint.

To draw is to measure, to lay down proportions of size. Since the coloured surface contains implicitly the measures and proportions of size, which the draughtsman produces explicitly, it follows that painting is a complete portrayal, drawing a partial one.

Let us try to realize the genesis of a large picture, an elaborate composition in the workshop of Rubens. The master drew 'from nature' figures in movement, on a small scale, and disregarding colour. He also 'out of his head' produced small sketches for the entire composition, adopting a colouring which was appropriate to the view from a distance. With the assistance of the drawings the composition, conceived on a small scale, was transposed by the master or the assistants into life size, and the colouring strengthened, adjusting it to the view from close by.

The standpoint is thus continuously shifted: visual impressions, received at varying distances, are combined, and with regard to colour there prevail convention, habit and routine. A picture such as the one now postulated—how utterly unspontaneously it originated, how heterogeneous it is, how definitely it did *not* spring out of one single visual experience! The masters drew 'from nature' and painted 'out of the head'. Recollection of that which had been seen was keener, better trained with regard to form than colour. One may say that for a long time painting was nothing but coloured drawing.

Painters of the 17th and 18th centuries overcame the conflict here alluded to up to a point—in a higher or lower degree according to their individual disposition and the tasks which they set themselves; Aelbert Cuyp more effectively than Ruisdael, Chardin more effectively than Watteau. Often the intellectually modest had, as painters, the advantage and led the way. It was left, however, to the unacademic Impressionists of the 19th century to settle the conflict completely, to overcome it deliberately.

Just as appearance in the practice of the school is divided up into form and colour, so is it possible again to differentiate between colour and tonality. It is true that we never perceive a coloured surface without a tonal value, which depends on the light. If we therefore speak of 'inherent colour'—local colour—we cannot by this understand anything else but colour placed under normal and uniform conditions of light.

Light may flare up in one place, fail in another, transform inherent colour and alter its nature. The green leaf on the tree looks white when touched by the light. In one place colour begins to glow, shows the maximum of its force; in another it is extinguished by the flood of shadows. In what we call *grisaille*-painting the inherent colour is completely negatived, and appearance reduced to contrasts of tonality. In *clair-obscur* painting, which triumphed in the 17th century, the artists one-sidedly and deliberately paid heed to lighting and, out of wilfully emphasized contrasts of light and shade, gained moving, dramatic and mystic effects. In doing so they ventured upon a subjective intervention, a violation which allows us to deduce that the painter's consciousness of his own worth had risen high. Splendour and charm of colour need not as a result be sacrificed: the colours may even gain in intensity through the contrast with the neutral masses of shade, and by being as it were set like jewels. The late works of Rembrandt offer a case in point.

If an objective interest in things prevails, then clear and complete information about the inherent colour and inherent form of things is asked for, and light with its capricious changes is felt to be a mischief-maker. An instructive instance is offered by Saenredam's pictures, if you compare them, say, with those of Emanuel de Witte. In the former the light is neutralized for the love of the factual data of architecture.

The function of light is a complex one. It makes the inherent colours 'light up', but in an extreme degree —be it strength or weakness—it destroys form as well as colour; it also yields colour—gold and silver. Bodies appear three-dimensional by not letting through the light. In this fashion light emphasizes the cubic illusion, and so gives greater depth to space. Finally light composes, since there exists a solidarity between beings and things in this, that they are made visible by the same source of light, that they, in a sense, owe their existence to it. The parts of a picture form a family from being the children of light. A consistent observation of lighting—a late conquest —came to replace the rhythmic disposition achieved by symmetry and equipoise.

A body which is placed against the light appears dark on one side—this is the shadow of the body itself. A shadow which lies outside the boundaries of the body is called a cast shadow. It displays at times a mirrored image of the body which intercepts the light, and is more or less distorted. It serves as a bridge between the body and the world around it. The shadow of the body itself satisfies the objective interest in things; the cast shadow, on the other hand—a mimicking addition, tail or train—tells you nothing about inherent form, but it does tell you about spatial connection and the source of light. Only at a late period was the cast shadow made to serve the ends of the effect of a picture. Because sunlight by day, in the open air, spreads a diffused luminosity and does not let the cast shadows appear very distinctly— by contrast to artificial light in dark rooms—did it come about that Northerners, especially Dutchmen, took the lead in observing cast shadows.

4. MASTER OF ALKMAAR
PANEL FROM THE SERIES OF THE WORKS OF MERCY
Amsterdam, Rijksmuseum
Early example of strongly developed cast shadow, 1507

WARM AND COLD COLOURS

Through rays which have been thrown back—reflections—the shadow of a body is partly made lighter. This phenomenon remained unnoticed for a long time, more particularly since it seemed to confuse rather than to clarify the information about cubic shape. The rendering of the reflections as a symptom of close observation may be followed in the Low Countries. Jan van Eyck, Dirk Bouts, Hugo van der Goes, and in the 16th century more particularly Jan Gossaert, turn their attention to this lighting at second hand. Stephan Lochner, the willing pupil of the Netherlandish artists, uses the light streak in the shaded portion to set off the body against the dark background.

We speak of warm and cold colours, as in music of the minor and major key. Where colours are concerned it is a question not of absolute differentiation but of something more or less. Red stands at one end of the scale, blue at the other. Among the red colours there are some which are warmer and others which are colder. The red of strawberries, scarlet and crimson are warmer than red lake and vermilion. Ice is white and blue, fire glows red. The sense of feel has given the sense of sight the terms. We say 'cold' of the appearance of the sky, of infinity, of distance, of everything bald and torpid; warmth is suggested by that which is near, which grows organically, which is filled with sap, which is alive.

Colours, according as to whether they belong to the

cold or warm category, act as symbols, and indeed direct upon emotion, not according to convention. The cool colours express remoteness, distance, transfiguration—also reserved dignity; the warm colours express nearness, seclusion, intimacy, earthly narrowness. That which is seen in the distance contains cooler colours than that which is seen in the vicinity. The Impressionists, who carried out their observations in the open air, favour the cool colours. In the choice of this or that key, race and individuality reveal themselves.

Here, as an instance, is a comparative table of painters who face definitely one way or the other, often as a reaction against accustomed tendencies:—

Cold	*Warm*
Piero della Francesca	Dirk Bouts
Hugo van der Goes	Titian
Greco	Pieter de Hooch
Vermeer van Delft	Kalf
Snyders	Adriaen van Ostade
Teniers	

Gold, regarded as a colour value, is a colour value of a special kind, fulfilling in a picture a different function from all others. It does not belong to the means by which the illusion of reality is conjured up; on the contrary, it is one of the means which remove the work of art from the sphere of earthly existence

and counteract illusion. The gilt background nega-
tives space. The precious metal—striking the highest
note of decorative splendour, mysteriously glistening
in dark churches—resembles solemn, wordless music.
The priceless matter becomes in the work of art a
symbol of that which is spiritual and lacks body.

The painted antependium and the altarpiece originated as substitutes for metalwork, and for this
reason long adhered to the high splendour and glitter-
ing magnificence of plastic decoration and enamel. In
North Italian painting of the 15th century, the influence which proceeded from Greek Icons may be
followed into the art of Carlo Crivelli by reason of the
accumulation of gilt decoration. The quantity of gold,
occurring in a devotional picture, betrays the degree
of conservative, hieratic spirit.

Step by step we may trace how gold is eliminated,
from a desire for the ordinary things of this world as
also for depth of space. Jan van Eyck and some Floren-
tines in the 15th century—thus the most progressive
forces—rejected the precious material as irreconcilable with their method of vision. The Germans
and the Venetians clung yet awhile to the traditional
vehicle of glorification and adornment. In the haloes
—whether shown as disks or rays—and in the ornaments on the borders of the draperies, gold still remained in considerable use in the 15th century. German painters about 1470 have, naïvely and illogically,
combined the landscape setting with a gilt sky space.

Altogether, every material in itself 'beautiful' became more and more neglected in serious art—in favour of the claims to achieve illusion—and given over to decoration and industrial art; as for instance silk, ivory, porcelain, gold, and silver.

At last, ejected from the surface of the picture, exiled as it were into the ante-room, gold encloses and frames the fragment of nature and separates art, born of spiritual conception, from our reality.

V

THE CONCEPT OF 'PICTORIAL'

WE have come upon the concept of 'pictorial' in the antithesis 'pictorial method of vision and the draughtsman's method of vision'. In English there exist, alongside of the term 'pictorial', certain expressions of cognate significance—notably 'paintable' and 'picturesque'; and these two are of value in coming to the rescue of 'pictorial', while at times 'paintable' and 'picturesque' may be used almost indiscriminately. Thus certain effects observable in the sky—with its play of mists, clouds and coloured spaces fading away imperceptibly—suggest both 'paintable' and 'picturesque'.

The concept changes, according as we link it antithetically with concepts connected with draughtsmanship, plastic art or mathematics. The contour, the outline can produce an effect which, relatively speaking, is picturesque. A jagged rock in the mountains is more picturesque than the Pyramids. Even in the domain of geometry is it possible to observe a more or less picturesque effect. The oval is more picturesque than the circle, the rectangle more picturesque than the square. Between two points there are innumerable distances, of which the shortest is the least picturesque. The unexpected, unforeseen form appears picturesque, it occupies the eye, spurs it to activity, rescues it from lethargy. As a witty remark affects the spirit, so does picturesque form—its zigzag silhouette, its unexpected turns and twists, its slanting, displaced boundaries, its interrupted flow—affect the eye. The eye, in being hunted to and fro, reminds the spirit of movement in the outer world. A form which shows the traces and results of active forces is felt to be a picturesque one. That which has come into being organically, has grown organically, is more picturesque than that which has been made by man: an apple, a tree are more picturesque than a billiard ball or a column. Genuine jewels are more picturesque than the flawless and uniformly coloured ones which are produced synthetically. The desire for the picturesque means thirst for nature, flight from the prison of common sense, delight in untamed wilfulness, in adventure, in licence, in the amusingness of the incalculable.

Nature adorns and decorates her creatures in the animal and vegetal domain. Growth shows itself in the yearly circles in a tree, in nodes, layers, or rows of dots. On the model of Nature's ornaments man has adorned his body, his garments, his tools, his buildings. Succession and repetition, as brought about by nature, do not show the dead and stiff orderliness which is achieved by the calculations and measurings of the human spirit, but a looser regularity, which appears picturesque alongside the one produced with ruler and compasses. And attempts to rival the art forms of nature in richness of phantasy never wholly succeed. You get an idea of this richness of phantasy when you reflect that no two people have the same fingerprint—that is, the same patterning of the skin. The individual is more picturesque than the typical: the human spirit, with its fondness for order, seeks refuge with rules and regulations.

The painter uses the brush, the draughtsman the pencil or the pen. The brush produces spaces and dots, the pencil lines. Method of vision and vehicle affect each other reciprocally.

Up to a point, the brush can draw and the pencil paint; namely, indicate spaces of a certain tonality, or suggest them by hatching. The natural function of the one vehicle is and remains, however, to part, to cut up, to divide; and of the other to unite and to collect.

The method of vision is linked up with the interests of the contemplative spirit. Drawing appeals to the one who turns his attention to things and organisms in the outer world, classified according to categories; who seeks to account for things, who aims at grasping in appearance that which is permanent, solid and constructive—at understanding its essence. Drawing means to gauge, to fix proportions, to abstract, to pass over, and to eliminate the confusing play of light and colour. Masters of an actively mascu-line disposition—conscientious, bent upon imparting instruction, severe, thoughtful, concerned with con-veying information, telling a story and achieving ex-pression—have been great draughtsmen. Naïve and sensual natures, of feminine receptiveness, may be found among the great painters.

The student begins by drawing, and so did the human race. Roughly speaking art has developed from drawing in the direction of painting: though many swervings from the main road may be noted. The method of vision becomes modified in accordance with ethnical character, climate and individual dis-position. It is often said that the Germans are prim-arily draughtsmen. But even the more generalized claim that the Teutons are draughtsmen, say by con-trast with the Latins, would be entirely mistaken. In the Low Countries the Teutonic Dutchmen display more sense of the pictorial than the half-French mas-ters in the Southern Provinces. The great English painters of the 18th century were indifferent draughts-men, which is all the more strange since as collectors they showed a profound understanding of the draw-ings by the Old Masters. The influence of climate, of the condition of the air, seems to be stronger than that of race. Amsterdam and Venice—the cities of the painters—lie by the water's edge. The East, where sensual, non-spiritual ornament ruled, appears as a fountain head of a pictorial method of vision. Venice lay open to impulses from the East; Greco came from there, *via* Venice, to Toledo, the half-Moorish city.

The favourite notion, that the artistic activity of nations and races from inherited disposition always follows the same direction, is often contradicted by observation. The French evince in the 12th century superior gifts for monumental sculpture. Then follow rather barren periods. In the 18th century the French lead the way as constructive draughtsmen; in the 19th they reach their zenith through their sense of nature and pictorial method of vision. The Germans, prominent as draughtsmen and engravers, are suddenly for a short time, through the work of Cranach, Altdorfer and Grünewald between 1503 and 1515, painters in the narrower sense of the word, and in a higher degree than the contemporary Netherlandish Masters.

VI

SIZE AND SCALE, DISTANT VIEW
AND NEAR VIEW

THE size of a painting, provided that the artist's choice has been spontaneous, tells us about the intentions, and hence about the individuality, of the painter. In many cases it is not a question of choice; the commission automatically settled the point in question. A space of wall of given dimensions had to be filled, an altarpiece of such and such a spatial extent was ordered. Latterly the painter has had relative freedom in his choice of size.

A reciprocal relationship exists between the spatial extent of the picture and its conception; and again between the latter and the manner of painting. Emotional and spiritual greatness widens the picture-space, narrowness of mind favours modest size and small scale. The large picture directs the spectator to a standpoint at some distance from the picture-surface, and forces the painter to change his standpoint, to step back in order to take in the whole and judge of the effect; it also makes it necessary for him to adopt a broad, quick, summary manner of painting. The little picture is, in itself, dainty; the large one monumental, whatever the subject. Every painter may, in accordance with his inclination, find a certain size convenient, welcome and pleasant, only in past centuries he was often obliged by action from the outside to avail himself of a size which was uncongenial to him.

The small size of the pictures by Dou appears natural, like the large size of the paintings by Tintoretto. To each size there corresponds a definite quantity of content of form. Hence each size demands a definite measure of knowledge of form.

Period, local conditions and tradition determine size and scale. The 16th century strove after monumentality with increased pretension and ambition, in comparison with the 15th century. To the Italians, schooled in wall painting, the large scale came more naturally than to the Netherlandish artists, whose panel pictures in the 15th century do not disown a descent from manuscript illumination. As late as the 17th century the Dutch felt most happy when painting a picture of small or medium size.

To each picture theme—within movable limits—a definite size is appropriate. Ostade's boors, on a life-size scale, would be unbearable. Potter's *Bull*, large as life, makes a grotesque impression. A painter of tact and self-discipline, like Gerard Terborch, clings with determination to the size which fits his talent, his method of painting, and his subjects like a glove.

SIZE AND SCALE

Apart from the compulsion springing from the order, ambition not infrequently entails discord, lack of harmony between size on the one hand, expressive power and method of painting on the other. Indissolubly connected with large dimensions is rhetorical pathos, which sounds hollow and disappoints the spectator, except when conception and expression are attuned to the size.

In the individual development of a painter one can notice the direction from small to great, presupposing that a strong talent is striving for release and that forces from the outside do not intervene with paralyzing effect. A genius struggles forward along this path even against the current of the time, as for instance Rembrandt in a period which chooses to move in the opposite direction. As they get more mature and older, painters gain an ever wider view, a sense of connection; they sacrifice details and become psychically far-sighted. Attention is turned from the leaf to the branch, from the branch to the tree, from the tree to the forest.

Rembrandt has at all times, in all the phases of his development, painted large and small pictures; in the early period conception and expression were such as befitted the small size, in the late period such as befitted the large size. In the early period a view from close on prevails, in the late period a view from a distance.

A human figure in the distance looks small. Since

we know its real size the one which we have noticed reveals to us its place in the depth of space. The figure in the distance, seen across dulling strata of air, loses some of its volume, its colour and its distinctness. Erroneously it might now be deduced that a figure, painted on a small scale, must show the characteristics linked up with the distant view. This is by no means the case. On the contrary the small picture attracts the spectator and pleases him by reason of its smooth technique, richness of detail and definiteness. Jan van Eyck painted on a small scale with a near view—a fact which we already noted when we remarked on the discrepancy between form and colour; Tintoretto on a large scale with a distant view. Jan van Eyck gives us a reduced near view, Tintoretto an enlarged distant view. A life-size near view—such as Leibl sometimes gives us—runs the risk of producing the effect of wax-works. Every painter gets accustomed—in conformity with his period and his individual bent—to a vision derived from a near view or a distant view, and he carries this out more or less independently of size and proportion.

Roughly speaking the evolution of painting moves from a near view towards a distant view. The primitive delight in splendid and positive local colours, the objective interest in things, which forbade the sacrifice of the facts of inherent form and inherent colour, were for a long time more authoritative than the logic of sight as conditioned by atmosphere and perspective. Up to a point the evolution of the individual corresponds to that of mankind.

The open, broad, bold method of painting, in contrast to the one which is firm and enamel-like, developed parallel with the transition to a distant view. One may compare for instance the stone walls in the pictures of Jan van der Heyden and Jan van Goyen. In one case the stones are indicated emphatically and accurately, they can be counted; in the other they are rendered by irregular, 'pictorially' lively brushwork, in their effect from afar. Jan van der Heyden of the near view was younger than Jan van Goyen. There was also such a thing as retrograde movement in the history of painting.

Atmospheric perspective cannot be calculated, or construed, like linear perspective. According to the distance from the eye and the condition of the air, colour is subject to alteration, becomes in the direction of depth, lighter, paler and more neutral: hence it has something to tell us about the locality of an object. The painter observes this fact, with the intention of arousing and emphasizing the illusion of depth of space. While, so far as linear perspective is concerned, he is tied by rules, he can treat atmospheric perspective with comparative freedom. In the 16th century, as depth of space was greeted with enthusiasm like a new discovery, the effect of the local position on the alteration of colour was often exaggerated, intentionally emphasized, schematized and distributed in degrees. Three zones were abruptly differentiated from one another. The first zone, in the foreground, was to be of warm brown colour; the second predominantly green; the third light, cool, blue. This tripartite disposition—carried out for instance in the landscapes of Jodocus Momper—gradually gave way to a more natural, imperceptible transition of the different grounds into one another.

Atmospheric perspective, as a compositional device, has, notably in the 19th century, been accentuated beyond a relation to observation, for instance by Corot, whose late manner is essentially based upon gradation of tone. A reaction against it has not failed to materialize.

Within the picture the zones of depth were fairly early—and particularly eagerly at the beginning of the 16th century in Holland—gradated in such a fashion that the larger figures in the foreground were done in conformity with a close view, and the smaller figures in the distance in conformity with a distant view. And the contrast strikes one at times as very abrupt, for instance in Pieter Aertsen's pictures.

VII

ON LINEAR PERSPECTIVE

PERSPECTIVE is, it seems to me, regarded one-sidedly in literature—as a method of subjective expression, as a conquest of spirit striving for order —and too little as a phenomenon having an objective existence. A philosopher may perhaps object that 'a phenomenon having an objective existence' is in itself a contradiction, but I hope the reader will understand what I mean. The boundary lines get displaced in accordance with the location of the object in the depth of space. The horizontal lines of the side wall of a cube—of which we know that they run parallel —converge towards one another. This strikes the eye independently of a knowledge of the laws of perspective, a knowledge which as a matter of fact, historically speaking, is a late discovery. The phenomenon was always visible, only it was not perceived. A painter who, wholly unfamiliar with the laws of perspective, shows us the saint large, the house at some distance behind him comparatively small, has already begun to see in conformity with perspective.

It is the subjective point of view of the spectator,

which decides whether, and how consistently, the modification of inherent form through displacement, foreshortening and overlapping is observed and realized in a picture. As long as a cube, independently of its accidental position, is the primary object of interest, its appearance in perspective can be rejected as a distortion, as an optical delusion, and wilfully corrected. Against the evidence of appearance, without taking any notice of it, one was capable of drawing the horizontal lines of the lateral space of the cube as parallels, as long as one gave more credence to knowledge than to seeing. This was the case when one aimed at showing in their inherent forms, and at reproducing, the individual object, the thing, the human figure, the beings classified according to concepts—without the least interest in spatial connection or the relation of the bodies to one another.

In Primitive Art, far into the Middle Ages, the proportions of size were determined less through observation than through a spiritual table of precedence. Godhead was honoured by size, the sovereign distinguished by size, the donor in prayer, the slave in his servitude depicted on a relatively small scale. Looking in amazement at such compositions people have come upon the questionable concept of the 'inverted perspective'—which has led to absurd deductions. As people began to ponder over the world around them and over structural surroundings, over the spatial relations that existed between the individual things.

E

some attention was given to perspective. Step by step it may be followed in examples belonging to the Middle Ages, how the draughtsmen rendered such or such a displacement due to perspective, with approximate correctness, at first purely on the evidence of their eyes. Early attempts at construing—partial and inconsistent—have, indeed, also been noticed. The thirst for space, which in the 15th century grew powerfully, increased the capacity for seeing in conformity with perspective. The need was present earlier than the understanding. Just as the wish to make books accessible to the many—even to the poor—released the thought of printing with movable letters, so did the thirst for space drive people on to the discovery of the laws of perspective. The decisive revolution, furthered by masters of genius like Jan van Eyck, preceded the successful geometrical construing. After the rules had been discovered, and as they were being learnt, everybody was capable of conjuring up the illusion of depth on the surface of the picture, and the trick was being practised with passion during the 16th century.

Art which decorates surfaces—I have in mind such categories as wallpainting, stained glass, vase painting, tapestry—observes, more or less at all stages of development, a discreet reserve as regards the phenomenon of perspective—from disinclination to pierce or destroy the wall or the vessel through arousing a strong spatial illusion.

THE MIDDLE AGES AND PERSPECTIVE

The Medieval master who painted an altarpiece had to adorn a piece of church furniture, and to show the congregation saints who do not breathe like human beings in such and such a room. Neither form nor spiritual content, therefore, directed him to aim at spatial illusion. Less as a result of immediate observation, than of visual knowledge, he took from natural appearance exactly as much as he needed for his purposes of decoration and the concretizing demanded by the cult he served. The phenomenon of perspective he did not require.

The painted panel originated in the Middle Ages as a substitute for precious panels in relief; and, in conformity with this, it remained for a long time tied to the laws of style which govern sculpture. Now to the sculptor it is something alien to see in accordance with the rules of perspective.

Painting in Asia, even in its finest performances, does not know that thirst for space, which in Europe led to the realization of the laws of perspective. Painting in Asia cultivates the flat surface and decoration. It has well been said that this kind of painting is essentially writing. If one considers artistic activity all over the world, one discovers that intensive interest in producing the illusion of depth of space is restricted to a relatively small field, both in time and space.

The development of European painting from the 15th century onwards may be regarded as a fight against the picture surface, and a glorious victory in the history of this campaign was the realization of the mathematical rules. The thirst for space belongs to the period of discoveries, a period during which the spirits of men longed to be different and elsewhere; a period of a generation energetic in its endeavour, eager for conquest and relentlessly pushing forward.

Labouring under a misapprehension, one has said of some great masters of the 19th century that they had renounced the method of vision which takes account of perspective. Notably Cézanne has been praised as a breaker of mathematical tables of the law. Such a view has this much truth, that depth of space, conquered and secured, no longer calls forth enthusiasm as a newly discovered land of wonders, and that the passion for a complete harmony of the picture-surface keeps artists from emphasizing the lines which create space, from elaborating depth of space wilfully. Appearance, idolized in the 19th century, is after all a matter of surface, and the objective interest in that which exists three-dimensionally has waned.

VIII

MOVEMENT

THE formative artist cannot represent movement, although he experiences it in his contemplation: he can only interpret it at second hand. The striving after movement is intense for more than one reason. Movement is life; it is the symptom of being alive, and it is the illusion of life with which art has been and is concerned. To give information about events and happenings entails a change of locality in the course of time, which confronts the artist with an insoluble problem. It is, indeed, the fate of the artist to find himself faced with insoluble problems.

Space and movement further each other mutually. The stronger the illusion of space, the more readily do the bodies seem to move in it. On the other hand the body in movement creates for itself space as the stage of its change of place. Even an object at rest, seen in conformity with perspective, creates in our imagination the space of which each object occupies a part. A body in movement widens space. A figure, turning round in dancing movement, emits space around itself. Walking, running, flying, the body suggests the

space that it has left, and the space which it will reach
—even beyond the frame; in this way it contributes
not a little towards making picture-space appear as
part of boundless space—and thereby towards making
the picture appear as something cut out of nature.

With movement, time, which is alien to the character of formative art, is so to speak introduced by
stealth: and the door is thrown open to narration, to
epic, to drama.

The pendulum of a clock hangs in one phase of its
oscillations in a perpendicular position, in all others
in an oblique position. Whoever tries, as best he can,
to render the swing of the pendulum in a picture, fixes
on the canvas any position of the pendulum except
the strictly vertical one. Why? Because the pendulum might be at rest in this but in no other position. Whoever will conjure up the appearance of
movement choses positions in which the body is incapable of remaining permanently. From the report
'this cannot last', we receive the information 'this is
in a state of transformation'.

Pictorial rigidity is to be conquered by cunning and
discretion. The goal is reached by a circuitous route.
If in reality I observe a man running or a bird flying,
and, with an intention of reproduction, try to impress
on my memory of forms some of the outlines which
show themselves in a continuous flow—cross-sections,
as it were, of extension in time—then distance favours
me more than vicinity, because the body moves—or

rather seems to move—more slowly the greater its distance from my eye.

A comparative lack of detail in the form enclosed by outline, predominance of the silhouette, neutralized local colour—these are characteristics linked up with a distant view. The more distant, paler, smaller, and more unreal a body in itself appears to be, the more easily does the impossible become possible—namely that it moves in the picture. If a master paints a running horse in each of two spatial zones of a picture —and each time with the content of form which strikes his eye at the distance concerned—then the small horse in the distance will produce a stronger illusion of movement than the large one in the foreground. And this is the reason why the masters, who most eagerly and successfully have gone in for movement, have shown a preference for small size and a sketchy, rapid handling—or even were draughtsmen or engravers, who were content with black and white, the convention which is a stranger to nature. I think, say, of Bruegel, Toulouse-Lautrec, or Slevogt. A check from the opposite angle is easy. In a wax-works a wax figure in real clothes, life size and then in an attitude of running would surely produce a ridiculous effect.

Generally speaking this law is valid: the more truth to nature is offered, the greater are the claims for even more of such truth. Illusion resembles the god that consumes his own children. The wax figure just referred to, so true to nature, produces an unnatural effect because it does not move; thus does not do what it ought to do in conformity with the intentions of whoever made it.

Let us compare the *Bull* by Potter—the life-size one in the Mauritshuis—with a bull by Rubens. The former has been intended for a near view, is true to nature in all its details, and bulky; the latter is seen from a greater distance, is poorer in detail, flatter in effect and partakes of the character of a vision. The former is a portrait; the latter more typical, with the characteristic qualities of this animal species. The latter moves, or at any rate appears capable of movement: the former, on the other hand, in spite of all naturalness of structure and texture, is without life and painfully stiff. Potter's bull seems to belong to the real bulls, of which we ask that they shall really move. Potter, the leading expert on the animal body, fails when he tries to depict animals in motion, more particularly on a larger scale.

There exist many devices for increasing the illusion of movement, and for strengthening the illusion of being alive; and all converge on the necessity of lessening the reality of a body in movement. We are unable to observe a moving body as closely as a body at rest. We lack the necessary time. Sympathetic apprehension of movement forces pencil and brush to quick action.

The opposite pole to the work of art is the 'living

picture'. While the work of art aims at illusion of reality, the 'living picture' is reality which conducts itself as a work of art. And the effect is painful, for reasons similar to those which cause us to be irritated by a wax figure.

The instantaneous photograph, the cinematograph, the slow-motion picture enable us to check the efforts of artists. The camera, thanks to the instantaneous photograph, seizes each and every phase, a thing which the human eye, experiencing the flow of movement, is unable to do. Slow motion shows this flow delayed, so that the eye is enabled to grasp picture phases with better success.

By means of the instantaneous photograph—however instructive and informative it may be—the longed-for illusion is not to be achieved. It gives less than is needed, because the eye cannot be so quick at the uptake as the camera; and more, because—as comparative checking proves—no instantaneous photograph achieves what the artist aims at. We see in a photograph too natural a horse, which leaps without being able to move from its place. In order to give the appearance of this 'moving from its place' the draughtsman employs devices which fall beyond the camera's range: he chooses a phase which communicates to the imagination of the looker-on the before and after—and thereby the flow of movement. No instantaneous photograph shows precisely such a phase. Even the quickest visual grasp is offered many forms of the body in a rush, but, strictly speaking, none is offered it. From his recollection of visual experience, and sympathetically apprehending action, the artist creates the form which is contained in no instantaneous photograph, yet conjures up the flow of movement more effectively than any such photograph.

Since it is the master who most inclines towards the dynamic—that is to say, towards what is essentially pictorial, the art of the brush—and who therefore aims above all at expressing movement; and since on the other hand movement is captured rather with pencil than with brush, we come up against an apparent contradiction which, however, settles itself when we consider how 'pictorially' the fanatics of movement—say Toulouse-Lautrec—draw, and conversely how closely akin to drawings are the paintings by Bruegel.

IX

TRUTH TO NATURE, ARTISTIC VALUE
AND STYLE

THE philistine finds it easy indeed to give reasons for his artistic judgment, and is accustomed to do it cheerfully, full of his own importance and without hesitation. He compares the artist's expression with nature—or rather with that which he has noticed or does notice in nature—and then proceeds quite unperturbed to decide on the value or otherwise of the rendering. A painter is blamed because he has produced a figure unnaturally long, a nose incorrectly drawn. The lover of art, who wishes to stress his distance from the misguided dry-as-dust spectator, is utterly disinclined to discuss such a thing as 'correctness'.

Yet it is impossible wholly to eliminate truth to nature in passing aesthetic judgment. Art, noble and free, has never, and at no stage of its development, been able to do without observation of appearances available to vision. Let us take the subjective as our starting point, namely, the wish and aim of the artist. He perceives what pleases him, and he wishes to seize it because it pleases him. Without question he desires to render it correctly.

An understanding between artist and spectator is only possible because both speak the same language—that is, in their vision have experienced the same from nature. However bold his imagination, the formative artist is thrown back upon nature. If we take a master like Greco, who from abnormal disposition did violence to natural forms, we can establish that there are limits even to so definite and furious an intervention. Bodies and hands, space and landscape, remain in any case within the domain of the recognizable.

Truth to nature is by no means everything, as the philistine fondly imagines: but it is *something* and it is indeed the *conditio sine qua non* for effect. Perhaps graphology may help to clear up the complicated relationship between accuracy and the artistic value which exists in formative art. A particular handwriting is not beautiful because the letters are shaped so as to be legible; but without such a condition it is impossible to admire the writing as beautiful, or full of character, or personal—in such a case it is nothing but meaningless scrawls, meaningless playing about. Similar considerations apply to formative art, which speaks to us by accustomed valid signs, by natural forms visible to all: just as a poem by Goethe consists of words which everyone uses. Michelangelo's *Moses* is monumental, powerful, mighty in its effect. If this work, however, no longer reminded us of the normal human body, which the artist has taken as his starting point, then we would be unable—by unconscious comparison—to feel the mightiness, the greatness. The superhuman is not to be expressed without the human.

Subjectively every formative artist is addicted to Naturalism; objectively he is less so, according as he produces visions which differ from common sights.

With painters, as is well known, you should not talk of photography. They fear a confusion and disclaim, often with suspicious violence, any interest in photography. It is not an accident that photography was born very nearly at the same time as the pictorial courage of the Naturalistic painters and the Impressionists. The camera produces a lasting reproduction which has not passed through a human being's head and brain: it is hence something new—nature's autograph.

A photograph is, however, objective only in a relative sense—namely, in relation to a work of art. The photographer too follows the dictates of individual taste, and is a child of his time. In the choice of subject, the standpoint, the particular detail singled out on the field of vision, the conditions of light, also in the focussing of the negative or the greater or lesser sharpness, there remains—entirely apart from retouching—considerable latitude for subjective intervention. Hence photographs reflect the style of pictures belonging to the same period.

Nevertheless, the photograph gives a standard, a reliable report, from which the artist can check his vision; and the photograph is not infrequently used, and misused, as the basis of artistic activity.

Now and then a painter on looking at a photograph from nature may exclaim in despair: 'If this is the result of all striving after truth then all our effort has been misdirected!' And perhaps the painter then turns to 'abstract art'. Such an effect has at times been promoted by photography, and it may be assumed that in future it will make itself felt even more strongly.

The optimist consoles himself with the reflection that since photography has taken over all the functions of the pictorial report, the complete satisfying of the objective interest in things, and grows more competent every day to discharge these functions, art can now retire to, and concentrate upon, the inner and real field of its activity.

If we confront the work of art with the photograph —say in order to prove errors which may be laid to the artist's charge—and assuming that we are concerned with a true and authentic work of art, then we find ourselves face to face with the personality of the author, his style, and, incidentally, perhaps also with the secret of artistic activity.

We say that this church is built in the Gothic style, this picture is painted in the style of the Dutch School of the 17th century, that picture in the style of Murillo. Work done by the hand of man reveals itself to the senses and to the spirit through its style, as having been produced at a certain time and a certain place, or by a certain master.

We use the expression with the intention of praise in cases where a personality, or the artistic endeavour of a period or a people, or a technical method, evinces itself in full purity and clearness, and moreover pervades the whole. Now since the word 'style' denotes something in the work of art that does not originate in existing reality, or at any rate indicates a visual experience given not to everyone but precisely to this one master, we are inclined to look upon style and truth to nature as opposed to one another. And this antithesis looms disastrously in writings on aesthetics. We must, however, sharply differentiate the subjective attitude of the artist from the result. Style is born at all times and everywhere, on individual formative power being exercised—even in cases where the artist gives himself up unreservedly to nature. Style is born, where wilful stylizing is by no means intended. Nay, perhaps we really ought to speak of style only when a work has come into shape, as it were, of itself on passing through the brain and heart of a human being. A conscious endeavour to purify, elevate and beautify nature leads to 'mannerism'. In any case style connotes producing *and* stylizing, that is to stamp form consciously in this or that fashion: it is of a definitely dual nature.

Drawing, with its emphasis of boundaries and its

79

renunciation of colour, can produce just as profound effects as painting. This alone indicates that closeness to reality does not exclusively supply the standard for judging the degree of merit of a work of art.

Engraving, woodcut and lithography stand in a closer and more convenient relationship to poetry, history, satire, and humour than painting. The circumstance that truth to nature is limited and lessened through technical vehicles and absence of colour allows of boldness and concretization of thought. There opens to the art of black-and-white a room for action—locked off from reality—in which imagination can indulge in free flights, without being hampered by demands for illusion and without being dragged down to earth.

The sculptor, in giving shape to the human body, favours materials which as regards colour and texture are far removed from the quality of human flesh, such as marble or bronze. This is done with instinctive, hence infallible, sense of style. Seldom and only exceptionally does he choose wax, a material which is relatively similar to flesh.

We admire the interpretation of soft flesh in the exquisite figure of Judith by Konrad Meit in the National Museum at Munich. The figure, carved in marble or alabaster, stands no higher than about six inches. If it were larger and, say, coloured its naturalness would produce a disagreeable effect.

The painter is not as anxiously afraid of confusion

with reality as the sculptor, if only because frame and flatness have the effect of barriers. But even he tries to evade nature with innocent cunning. Thus *clair-ob-scur*, which was developed by the 'Naturalistic' painters of the 17th century with such fanaticism, was a counterpoise to the pitiless sharpness of the observation of nature, to the brutal closeness to the individual model in the figures. The ascetics of Ribera have need of the mercifully concealing action of night, which with its pathos offers a substitute for that idealism which is wanting in the figures, with their prosaically portrait-like character. Rembrandt's *clair-obscur* signifies an escape from the commonplace luminosity of everyday life.

Two forces produce dynamic tension in the work of the formative artist: consciously, a never satisfied impulse to get to close grips with nature; and, subconsciously, a fear to come too close to her. When that fear penetrates from subconsciousness into consciousness, an unfortunate situation arises. Goethe, in saying 'There is no surer way of evading the world than through art and no surer way of linking up with the world than through art', may not have had exactly in mind the antinomy here formulated; but I am unable to refrain from quoting phrases which provide an apparent confirmation.

A gifted but inexperienced draughtsman who, with a naïve sense of his own worth and with praiseworthy intentions, sets about to reproduce nature, becomes desperate as a hailstorm of impressions descends upon him. The chapter in Gottfried Keller's novel *Der grüne Heinrich*, describing what happened to the boy as he tried to draw a tree, is more instructive than aesthetic treatises. The educational curriculum of the artist in the past, and up to a point even now, brings it about that the student seldom experiences that wholesome failure which Keller has described so graphically. This is because—by copying and imitating—he has absorbed into his visual memory, and carries with him, those comprehensible formulae of art which correspond to his powers of expression: into these formulae, as into a narrow river bed, he canalizes the savage torrent of his impressions of nature. He often steps from the school of art into life precocious and foolhardy.

There used to exist recipes and rules, say, for the painting of foliage. And while we smile at such a pedantic degeneration of academic instruction we must yet, on unprejudiced examination of free, independent, 'Naturalistic' production, and not without amazement, pronounce it to be the case that every master has sought safety from the rising flood by withdrawing into a narrow home of his own. Weak and dependent artists evade disturbing nature by finding refuge in houses ready-made, self-contained and built by predecessors.

To emphasize one's personal style means to make a virtue of necessity.

THE ARTIST AND NATURE

The artist is in love with nature, not, like the dilettante or the virtuoso, with art. The more passionately he presses his suit, the more vigorously does he push individually differentiating forces—sprung from his own bent—out into the light, and stylizes—against his will. Only the virtuoso and the dilettante work to their own satisfaction; the artist never loses the feeling of standing before an insoluble task. 'Him I love, who asks for the impossible.' It is love of this kind that the artist may claim.

If he imagines that he has reached his goal, he has really come to the end and stands at that boundary where mannerism begins.

X

INDIVIDUALITY AND TYPE

MAN, the most significant item among those with which formative art concerns itself, occurs in real life as an individual; that is, physically and psychologically as a creature with unique qualities. There do not exist people who are identical. Individual character is the hallmark and symptom of the more highly developed creature. As formative art strove to produce an illusion of life, it made the eye more keenly observant of that which is individual. It was attracted by the individual shape, but also repelled by it. That which was individual appeared common, accidental, not corresponding with any concept or ideal. In order to give shape to gods and demi-gods, the artist was called upon to give life to ideals, through observation, without lowering them or distorting them. Thought conduces to type, as observation conduces to individuality.

Later, as painting was emboldened to mirror life on this earth, the relationship to individual appearance became modified. The qualities of inadequacy and faultiness, which attach to the individual being, gave no offence. But what was it all about, say, in the *genre* painting of the 17th century? The peasant, the cavalier, the housewife were to appear; customs and manners of a community, a society, a class were to be shown.

Interest was not taken in the peasant named Willem Muller—or it was taken only to the extent that he was a characteristic specimen. This intention conduced to category, and thereby once again to type. The smaller the scale, the easier was it to achieve satisfactory lifelikeness, without strong individualization. A small figure in the distance shows that which is typical; a large figure in a near view that which is individual. Ostade's boors all resemble one another. Jan Steen individualizes in a higher degree, more particularly when painting on a large scale.

Portraiture is definitely conducive to observation of the individual case.

Roughly speaking, the trend of development runs from the typical in the direction of individualization: but the goal is never reached. Something is always offering resistance. Thought—making for order—and judgment lead on to category.

The deeper we descend into the realms of creation, the less developed do we find individuality. In an animal, in a plant, we only notice that which is characteristic of the species.Man alone, among all creatures, shows himself a unique individual being. One may recognize in it an advantage and the 'crowning happiness of earth's children' (Goethe). There is, however, a standpoint from which individuality is recognized in the aesthetic sense as something which is ugly ethically, as a curse in the Christian sense, as a consequence of the Fall of Man, as something which is unredeemed. And in order to understand the extent to which artistic activity is dominated by religion, one ought to approach this standpoint.

XI

ON BEAUTY

THE concept of beauty suffers from an ominous generalness and painful vacuity. We call beautiful that which pleases the eyes, which we look at with pleasure. Pleasure, however, offered by nature, is different in kind from the sense of pleasurableness engendered by art. That which pleases us, as embodied by the artist, can displease in nature, nay prove unbearable. Since beauty in nature and that which has value in art are divergent, we feel inclined to avoid the expression 'beauty' in judging of art. It would however be a mistake simply to exclude from the domain of art beauty in nature—that is healthy fairness of form, gracefulness of movement, regular features, charm. But the relations between beauty in nature and artistic value are complicated.

To begin with, our judgment on beauty in nature is dependent on our experiences of art. After all, it is from artists that we have learnt to appreciate beauty in nature.

That which in life gives us a sense of happiness, through form, colour and movement, is something which we do not by any means seek to find again in pictures. Beauty in nature is no indispensable condition for artistic production; but it does supply the artist with a device. In a picture it symbolizes a noble, lofty mind, purity of soul, innocence, saintliness. As a sensual attraction it also operates in the context of mythological or bucolic subjects.

Physical beauty in a picture is something typical and not individual. This is confirmed by the examination of works which we owe to masters thirsting for beauty, such as Raphael, Correggio or Watteau, and also to the Greek sculptors.

The more pronouncedly individual a human being appears, the more imperfect does he seem. One can look upon every individual creature as an attempt that failed. The formative artist is faced with the alternative of sacrificing either fairness of form or truth to nature; and as long as he had to provide pictures of gods and saints, his choice was prescribed to him. Later, the cleavage between beauty and truth became increasingly wider.

People have been fond of romancing about great masters who derive their ideal of beauty from the face of a beloved woman. That this should have happened is perfectly possible, but the painter concerned must have modified the existing forms, consciously or unconsciously. If the Sistine Madonna resembled a woman who lived in Rome about 1520, then she would not be a Madonna; and if the Roman woman resembled the Sistine Madonna, then she would lack full power of life, nay the possibility of existence. Beauty in nature is provided for us in individual form and we demand it, because we demand life; but in a picture it produces a sense of tedium, because it is here devoid of breath and movement. The artist who avails himself of well-proportioned limbs and fairness of face for purposes of glorification, transfiguration and sanctification, has no use for that which is individual, since he must fear that it would bring his creations down to the imperfection and transitoriness of the earthly sphere. Everything individual calls to mind change and decay; that which is typical assures us of permanence and inviolability. No artist faces reality with such fastidiousness as the artist who strives for beauty. No artist strives less for beauty than the one who is in love with nature. Indifferent artists try to derive an advantage from the beauty of their subject.

It was left to some 19th century painters, lacking in instinct and ill-advised, to paint Madonnas with lovely women as their models—and with deplorable results.

The portrait of a lovely woman, *ceteris paribus*, is not superior as a work of art to the portrait of an ugly old man. To expect a maximum of artistic value if a great master paints a prize beauty, is nonsense, as everybody sees.

However trite the expression 'beautiful' may have become, even the nicely differentiating lover of art will always be driven by necessity in the decisive moment to go back to a word which, in spite of its emptiness *qua* thought, is highly saturated with feeling.

That which is unbeautiful, and repels in reality, is by no means excluded from formative art. Its functions are many. It increases by contrast the loveliness and charm of that which is well proportioned. It is used as a symbol for what is low, ignoble, evil. The desire for change is conducive to irregular formations since there exists but one norm, but the deviations from it are many. Ugliness is manifold, and hence 'picturesque'. Fate, or mental suffering, disfigure and distort fairness of form; increasing age consumes it. The wish to create, to scourge, and to deride characters; to indulge in pictorial humour or pictorial witticism: many such intentions impel the painter in the direction of the unbeautiful and make it picture-worthy.

Masters who keenly observed that which is individual, but were unable to free themselves from that which is conceptually typical, pushed forward to caricature, to the ideal of that which is mis-shapen—Leonardo or Quentin Massys, for instance.

XII

ON COMPOSITION

TO the eye there is displayed a confused and inarticulate juxtaposition of things; and to put this into order is the task of the human spirit. The painter told a story, reported, reproduced and strung together the picture parts, aiming at achieving a lucid, intelligible, limited whole. That which is visible is part of infinity: through being taken out by the artist it becomes something finite and entire.

The picture-space contains fields which, differing from each other in value, occupy as it were more and less honourable places. The middle appears as the distinguished position, and towards the sides the importance of the locality grows less. The severe symmetry of the primitive devotional image corresponded with the natural inclination to put the chief accent on the centre, and to strengthen the middle axis through the equipoise of the side portions. In the Northern wing-altarpiece this system of form corresponds with pictorial content. Symmetry—more and more loosened, it is true—rules throughout the design at all times. The need of it became paralysed through the striving after naturalness, after picturesque wealth of movement, after variety. Symmetry was felt to be something stiff and monotonous. Whoever traces the development of composition through the centuries, witnesses a struggle against geometrical regularity, and the duration of this struggle betrays that the scheme to be overcome put up a stout resistance. In a thousand variations of the lifeless arrangement—variations which give the appearance of an accidental juxtaposition—symmetry still remains operative, even when it is evaded. The accomplished compositions of Raphael convey the impression that the actors spontaneously, from a sense of noble and pious decorum, from a feeling of precedence, have arranged themselves in well-balanced groups. The happy marrying of articulating and organizing compulsion to inner freedom may be the basis of the unique perfection which is felt to be classic, and which is also characteristic of Greek reliefs.

Ever since the 15th century, depth was reckoned with in an increasing degree. The less the picture-surface was regarded as a space to be decorated, the more did the central axis lose in importance. While in the composition, based on the flat surface, vertical and horizontal lines predominated, the painters of the 16th and 17th centuries, by means of diagonal, of oblique disposition of the masses, aimed at variety and in particular at movement against the direction of the picture plane.

5. DIRK BOUTS, THE LAST JUDGMENT

Detail. Lille, Museum

Early example of a principal figure seen from the back, about 1460

TREATMENT OF HUMAN FIGURE

As a symptom of the change in the method of vision and—in connection therewith—in the composition, we must regard the human figure which turns its back on us. In Primitive art, and far beyond it, everything was concentrated upon man: to show him in the completeness of his physical structure was eagerly demanded, and in this connection only the full face and profile aspects were taken into account as decent, clearly informative, and dignified. Just as a tree or a house was not displayed in a bird's-eye view, so would a human being not be shown seen from the back. (By the way, Goethe strictly forbade his actors to turn their backs on the spectator.) A tremendous revolution was needed before a painter dared to present nothing but the back of a human figure. Early examples of such a bold enterprise may be found in works of Ouwater and Dirk Bouts, those two masters who came from Haarlem and worked about 1460. The figures which are turned away from us create the depth of space towards which they are turned, and increase the impression of accidental naturalness in an event or a situation which exists for itself and has not been got up for the spectator.

In the 17th century the illusion of spatial depth was vehemently demanded. Composition had to be subordinated to this demand. Heavy masses were disposed along the lower edge of the picture, or emerged from the foreground at the sides, acting as a *repoussoir* and causing the distance—a relative one—to appear airy and luminous by contrast. Enclosed by wings at the sides, the 'empty' centre gained a new importance, because it opened itself like a door towards infinity.

It was the endeavour of the painters subtly to modify and to conceal a method of disposition which was based on the laws of mechanics. They strove to get away from architecture, to whose severe closeness of construction they had formerly been subordinated. Not infrequently the art of composing consisted in concealing the action of composing. A construction which places that which is light, luminous, loose on that which is heavy, dark and solid; which places that which is borne on that which bears; that is what reason demands. But the delight in 'picturesque' freedom offered resistance to the basic principles of the building spirit. Picture composition in its evolution allows us to witness a struggle, in which the preference for natural caprice gradually became more and more victorious over mathematical regularity.

The consistent Impressionists no longer link up the parts of a picture into a whole, so that their intervention seems to be limited to the selection of the standpoint.

The function of the frame consists in this, that it assures us of the wholeness of the composition and encloses the work of art, isolating it. Pictures have at all times been framed, even if the manner in which this was done has varied. The wall painting, like any picture adorning a flat surface—also the colourless drawing—requires only an enclosing rim of slight strength, if any ending at all. The stronger the illusion of reality conveyed by a picture, the more insistently does the latter demand a frame—not one into which it may merge as a tapestry merges into its border; but a frame which, in colour as well as plastically, will stand out against the picture surface in clear contrast.

The harmony between picture and frame has in recent times been completely eliminated. It seems as if the frame proclaims, with exaggerated loudness, that the thing isolated within its limits is not reality, but a picture. In the 18th century, the frame was scarcely yet part of the picture: it was rather a bridge, which connected it with furniture, wall-decoration and architecture, and sprang from the same conception of taste.

The indifference with which the painters in the 19th century allowed their pictures to be framed produces a sense of distrustfulness. An amateur from the Far East is likely to find the styleless, haphazard, purely decorative gold fillets in which pictures are shown with us, simply barbarous. And it is hard to rebut such a taunt. As a matter of fact nothing is so compromising a revelation of the dissolution of expressive power throughout the whole domain of formative art than the inability—nay, the unwillingness—to produce a type of frame which would be appropriate to, and worthy of, the great painting of the 19th century.

Schinkel's enterprise, to put all the pictures of the Berlin Gallery into a uniform frame, allows us still to guess at a wish to bring the artistic contents into some connection with the museum building. It is not without a sense of shame that we look upon the wavering between anarchy and uniformity and turn admiringly to the past, in which picture and frame formed a whole, an organic unity, and the moulded fillet was subtly adapted to the picture space, heightening or supplementing the effect—differently in each case; now treating the frame simply, now with great complexity; making it a continuation and a barrier at the same time.

Efforts in recent times to invent frames 'correct in style' have been rather unsuccessful and often embarrassing. The modern picture must for the most part appear in old-fashioned get-up in order to be welcomed as something valuable and precious.

XIII

ON THE PICTURE CATEGORIES

IN conformity with a division according to the contents, the subject, the picture categories came into
being in the course of historical evolution. They are
rooted more or less deeply in the soil of ecclesiastical
art and allow us at the beginning of their growth to
recognize their origin from a stiff dignity and seriousness.

We may make the division as follows:—

I. *Altarpiece and Devotional Picture.*
(This includes the rendering of divine or holy
beings — existing and claiming veneration —
either singly or in rows or groups; also the
narration of legends and the illustration of the
Scriptures.)

II. *Pictures whose subjects are drawn from Myth, Fairy
tales, Poetry, History.*
(Imaginative invention adds allegory and apotheosis to myth; and it may be noted that events
from historical periods have mainly been depicted with an informative intention only from
the 19th century onwards.)

III. *The Genre Picture.*

(This includes the rendering of everyday occurrences originating in customs, work, family life, festive occasions.)

IV. *The Landscape Picture.*

(This includes the rendering of animals in the open.)

V. *The Architectural Picture.*

(This includes the city *veduta* and the interior of a building.)

VI. *The Still Life Picture.*

VII. *Portraiture.*

(This includes the single portrait and the portrait group; the rendering of individuals without any intention of producing a portrait; and heads done as studies.)

That which is visible, in its complexity combined with homogeneousness, resists being divided up according to concept; hence the boundaries between the picture categories are in a state of flux.

A Manet gives us details cut out of life, with no other intention than that of realizing a unique visual experience: with the result that his works—apart from his portraits—do not seem to belong to any category. To us such a mode of procedure appears so much a matter of course—indeed, the only duty of painting —that we take into consideration far too little the circumstances which in past centuries directed the will of the painter. A tendency, issuing from the 'What' of the rendering, determined, differently in each picture category, the 'How', with a vigour of compulsion which has become alien to us. Manet takes up his standpoint with regard to the whole of nature and life as the portraitist has done at all times with regard to his sitter. Everything that Manet has produced is, in a wider sense, a portrait, to the extent that one can paint portraits of flowers, fruit, houses and trees. And in this way we come to a provisional end and result of the evolutionary process.

In sketching the rise of the picture categories in the chapters which follow, I produce the evidence for my statements, since the considerations of principles which I have just set out will be, at any rate to some extent, confirmed, and indeed supplemented.

XIV

RELIGIOUS AND SECULAR HISTORY IN PAINTING

THAT which was considered and up to a point is s
considered as 'noble' art concerns itself with
'subjects of great significance to mankind'; and
long periods of time these are supplied by religion
myth. Now, for instance, the *Death of Wallenstein* is
unique and significant event, as is the *Procession to C
vary*. The advantage lies, however, with the histor
picture devoted to a religious subject, for more t
one reason. To start with, it is at once comprek
sible; it impresses devout Christians immediately
symbol. Moreover, tied to a long chain of traditi
the artist draws from a source of strength which d
not exist when he paints the *Death of Wallenstein*
which case mere poetry and bookish learning prov
a poor substitute for pictorial tradition. As a mat
of fact the most admired and permanently valid wc
of art are modifications and paraphrases rather t
inventions—Goethe's *Faust*, for instance. The grea
artists do not reach the summit by flight: on the c
trary, they move upwards on trodden paths until t
cover the very last distance on untrodden ones.

DIFFICULTIES OF HISTORICAL SUBJECTS

History, which is not sanctified and spiritualized by faith, offers subjects which are not easily mastered. Historical knowledge and patriotic enthusiasm lag behind when it is a question of depth, width and duration of effect. The picture in itself is silent. It is as an illustration—where the text gives information about that which is visible—that it can penetrate most successfully into the domain of poetry. Its real function is description of that which is known, not narration of that which is unknown.

Painting of subjects of secular history in the 17th century, as handled by Rubens, is not objectively informative or carried out in the spirit of the chroniclers. Even a Rubens, boldly and unhesitatingly mingling history, myth and allegory, can have achieved full comprehension—and consequently immediate effect —only with his patrons, say the princely house which he glorified. To our eyes, it is true, the decorative splendour remains sufficiently admirable in itself. In the domain of the decorative, for that matter, enigmatic quality and obscureness of subject are at home: indeed, they may at times have provided a stimulus of attractiveness, as for instance in the historiated tapestries of the 16th century, which scholars were wont to explain, subtly and entertainingly, to the princely patrons.

There is much which can yet be brought up against the historical picture. The mere fact that it is only the painters of the 19th century who have taken to this field, pretentiously and with an ambition directed towards the monumental, may be regarded as a suspicious symptom.

If I see a lady of fashion at her toilette, in a picture by Terborch, I am capable of finding delight in the carpet rendered in a masterly fashion. But whoever paints the *Death of Wallenstein*, and in this connection claims my attention for the design of a carpet, is not the man from whom I want to hear something about the fate of Wallenstein. Even theatrical producers have gradually come to see this.

'Historical accuracy', as to which some painters, like Piloty and Alma Tadema, indulged in so many illusions, is at all times only capable of convincing the artist's contemporaries, who know equally much or equally little. But entirely apart from the fact that accuracy of portraiture and costume is not to be achieved, it is not even desirable: for it lessens the sense of sublimeness through which alone the rendering of historically important happenings is justified. In the case of an event which took place centuries ago, it is only its effect in its historical context, and, say, the tragic destiny of a great personality, which can claim still to be alive in our imagination—certainly not costumes—and again definitely something spiritual, which the formative artist cannot immediately express. De-realization, removal from its chronological surroundings, apotheosis—that is what the imaginative artist will aim at in order to overcome the

6. ADOLPH VON MENZEL
SCENE FROM THE LIFE OF FREDERICK THE GREAT
Woodcut, about 1840

THE CASE OF MENZEL

unyielding qualities of the historical picture. What was the cause of the failure of the wretched historical painters of the 19th century? They aimed at greatness and dramatic effect, but simultaneously at reality in the highest possible degree. They painted John Huss at the stake, the executioners and the deeply moved spectators—from studio models. Pathos killed naturalness, and naturalness pathos.

But Menzel? This is a special case. Menzel was something like an investigator, operating with a drill bore. Also the King whom he depicted was, both in space and, relatively speaking, also in time, close to him. Finally: he was partly—and that part was not the worst one—an illustrator.

XV

THE NUDE

THE nude cannot strictly be regarded as a picture category, but asserts itself from the 15th century onwards, especially in the South of Europe, so insistently that the subject of a picture often appears to be merely an excuse to paint, or an opportunity of painting, disrobed people. Nudity is timeless, because every cloaking of it assigns to the figure its place in time; nudity is primary and perfect. God made the body, man the garment. This is the view which prevails ever since the Renaissance and dominates the imagination of formative artists. Nowadays, at a period when physical exercises are eagerly practised, we regard nudity as that which is natural: formerly it denoted the sublime and, earlier still, that which is devilish. Morality, as dictated by religion, could not be separated from aesthetics, and a Christian could not regard the body, burdened with hereditary sin, as 'beautiful'. More particularly in the North of Europe nudity remained connected with fear of witchcraft.

When artists in the 15th century began to notice that only knowledge of the nude made the appearance

7. ALBRECHT DÜRER, A NUDE WOMAN
Drawing. Bayonne, Museum
A transcript direct from nature, 1493

of the clothed figure comprehensible, keen attention was devoted to the organism at work beneath the clothing, and also to the skeleton at work beneath the flesh. Simultaneously, and in reciprocity with this endeavour, pagan sculptures were unearthed and attracted admiration as authoritative models. In this way prejudices crept in, and also something of the stylistic character of sculpture, inasmuch as the nude body engaged imagination less in flesh and colour than in hard, cold, colourless stone. *Contrapposto* attitudes of classical statues, and illusions as to measure, law and rule —guided by which the revered ancients were supposed to have shaped the beautiful and normal body —confused the spirits and drove them away from observation of nature.

Dürer never again rendered the nude body with such lack of prejudice as in his youth. The honest, 'unbeautiful' sketch of a nude woman which he drew in 1493 may be compared with late results of his untiring endeavour to gain the mastery of the unclothed human body. The ideal was conveyed along curious paths. The Greeks had been misunderstood by the Romans, as the Romans were by the Italians, and again the Italians by the Northerners.

In the 17th and 18th centuries study of the nude model—alongside of drawing from plaster casts—was introduced into the academic curriculum, in which connection admiration of classical sculpture made its influence felt more or less decisively. The nude body did not appear as innocent in the North as in the South. Lewdness with bad conscience crept into artistic expression, and instead of natural nudity the stripped body was shown. Study of the nude caused a shudder, more particularly in puritan countries, and contributed to detach the artists from ordinary society, to give them a sense of freedom which now and then degenerated into debauchery.

The study of the human body was carried out in conformity with the maxim 'divide and learn': it was studied first in its nudity, then draped in garments. The duality thus engendered is regrettably present all through artistic activity, to the extent that it was unable to free itself from the scholasticism of the academies.

It is with approval that we read the phrases of condemnation which Diderot addressed to the academic methods of instruction—notably as regards the drawing from the nude model and the study of anatomy. Goethe, who considered the French writer's *Essai sur la peinture* so valuable that he translated it and published it with critical annotations, contradicts the passionate 'Naturalist' with a sense of superiority, endeavouring to fix the boundary between art and nature and defending rule, law and theory. He remains, however, at some disadvantage, since Diderot takes as his starting point the consciousness of 'good painting', a consciousness which the German lacked. And the emotional life of painters, at least, was more familiar

8. ALBRECHT DÜRER, ADAM AND EVE
Drawing. New York, Morgan Library
The proportions construed; study for the engraving
Adam and Eve, 1504

to the enthusiastic lover of art than to Goethe, who looked upon paintings with the coolness of a judge. Diderot knew and loved at any rate one real painter, namely Chardin.

XVI

'GENRE' PAINTING

GENRE painting—which grew up late as an independent category of art—is, in the first instance, determined by the standpoint which the master has taken up with regard to life; and only in a secondary degree, by the situation which is shown in the picture, or the event which is narrated. Up to a point every occurrence can be apprehended from the point of view of *genre*. *Caesar crossing the Rubicon* is, to be sure, the subject for a historical picture, but only to the extent that the painter, who develops this episode in his imagination, is acquainted with the greatness of Caesar and the important consequences of his action, and, from such acquaintance, interprets the event in an heroic key. An innocent observer would perceive Roman soldiers who are getting across a river—thus a scene of *genre* character. A peasant sowing is undoubtedly the subject for a *genre* picture. Jean-François Millet, from his idea of the sanctity of work on the land, raises it, however, into the sphere of the religious. In itself, nothing possesses the character of *genre* or history: it is thought which produces that character.

Historical painting concerns itself with that which has happened once and at a given place; *genre* painting with that which every day happens here.

Genre-like motifs are to be found in abundance in the ecclesiastical art of the Middle Ages. Notably in the pictures of the months in the books of hours opportunities were provided for pictures of manners and customs. In the 16th century the *genre* picture separated itself, as an autonomous category, from the devotional picture, and did so at first shyly. Motifs from everyday life, which had crept into the religious pictures, push themselves audaciously into the foreground—for instance in the works of Pieter Aertsen —or legitimize themselves through a moralizing tendency. *Genre*, which had arisen in the devotional picture in contrast to that which is noble, holy or fair in shape, retained for a long time an inclination towards distortion and deformation. The *genre* picture suffered from the caricature as from an infantile disease.

In the 17th century, when *genre* painting blossomed forth and split into branches superabundantly, notably in the Low Countries, an optimistic view of the world, a youthful satisfaction with our present life, provide the foundation for an observation which penetrates into every nook and corner of existence. That which had been considered as an earthly vale of tears presented here and now an exhilarating aspect. Pictures which show us merry company and gay drinking bouts praise life as a festival, the earth as a pleasant dwelling-place. Especially in the Northern provinces, the Dutch Free State, did one contemplate with a sense of happiness the conditions of security obtaining in the narrow homeland, so victoriously defended and now enjoying the benefits of peace.

Political and economic causes account for the incredible extent and complexity both of content and form of the artistic production. On the sociological conditions under which the Dutch easel picture blossomed forth, a volume by Hanns Floerke may be consulted.[1]

Not princes, not the Church, not a princely Court, not individuals, distinguished and rich patrons—no, a people, a large number of well-to-do burghers, determined with their inclinations, wishes and taste the artistic activity. A completely secular character was here more easy of attainment than in the Catholic South, since, as a result of the puritan iconoclasm proclaimed by religion, the tradition of form had been interrupted. Moderately priced pictures in tremendous number, mostly of small or medium size, found their way to modest dwellings. Here for the first time did painting assume that *bourgeois* character which later became distinctive of modern art generally speaking. It is true that it is impossible, on political,

[1] Hanns Floerke, *Studien zur niederländischen Kunst- und Kulturgeschichte* (Munich, 1905).

sociological or philosophical grounds, to account for the abundance of talents which satisfy the requirements of a new stratum of society.

The real theme of *genre* painting is condition, not event. It is true that sometimes a descent is made upon the domain of the anecdote or short story—with particular gusto, for instance, by Jan Steen. Vermeer, however, and Gerard Terborch are, as narrators, reserved and still-voiced. That Goethe could interpret the so-called 'Fatherly Admonition' by Terborch so utterly wrongly allows us to realize how undemonstratively the painter told his story.

Modestly and contentedly comfortable, one only wished to see oneself, one's family, one's doings, one's possessions, one's house, one's garden, one's country in the mirror of 'good painting'. And since accuracy and knowledge of facts belonged to good painting, purpose—namely, the provision of satisfaction of the objective interest in things—and means—namely, good painting—coincided happily.

It is mostly a contemplative restfulness which prevails in the *genre* picture, as in Adriaen van Ostade's mature works and in those of Pieter de Hooch. The atmosphere of the day of rest is favoured. The peasants are not shown working on the land, but smoking and drinking in the tavern. To the extent that people act, they do what they do regularly and continuously, they do what they are accustomed to do. Only actions of that nature could count on immediate comprehension. The housewife looks after her child, the lady is at her toilette or makes music or writes a letter, the peasants drink, smoke or come to blows, the soldier plunders, the child is at play. It is always that which is typical, characteristic of the particular stratum of society, that is perceived—thus, that which is human in a general sense, and *not* indeed that which is unique. People appear not as individuals but as representatives of their rank, profession, sex, age. Terborch, who as regards stylistic instinct is superior to all his rivals, individualizes hardly at all in his *genre* pictures, and that in spite of his being an excellent portrait painter.

The *genre* picture, within its securely drawn boundaries, existed strictly speaking only in the 17th century and in the Low Countries. Later and elsewhere it changes like the chameleon, becomes bucolic, erotic, decorative, illustrative, sentimental, satirical, merges with the historical picture—in brief, it loses its self-contained, self-supporting character. The emotional colour which befits the *genre* picture is gay and in humorous agreement with that which is customary and belongs to every day. Humour is missing in the Italian and Spanish *genre* pieces, which, often in a sullen tone, speak of poverty and need, and, moreover, frequently—losing harmony with the subject—resort to the emphasis implied by the large size and the large scale of the figures.

9. JAN VAN EYCK, THE ROLLIN MADONNA
Detail. Paris, Louvre
Approximately half the size of the original

XVII

LANDSCAPE

O F the nature of Primitive art one can learn a great deal by speaking to children, observing their playful activities, and making experiments with them. If I ask a child to draw a landscape, it will be embarrassed and fail me; if on the other hand I suggest that it should draw a tree, it will eagerly set to work. What a child perceives, recognizes, absorbs into his pictorial memory are *things*. By 'things' I would like here to be understood a whole which exists in significant contours and may be singled out. In the first instance man is a thing in this sense, and, as Primitive art almost exclusively had to do with creatures moving about freely, it recognized nothing as picture-worthy except the self-contained bodies, and, weighted down by millennial traditions, it gained no access to landscape.

A mountain, a river are not 'things': at least they cannot be perceived as such and conveyed from their natural context into the pictorial context. The mountain is a tumefaction on the surface of the earth, the river a trench, filled with water, in the surface of the earth. In Cennini, who instructively hands on the view of the Italian Trecento, we read: 'If you wish to acquire a good manner of depicting mountains, and make them look natural, get some large stones, which should be rough and not cleaned, and portray them from nature, applying the lights and darks according as reason permits you.'

In order to represent mountains, a stone—which is a 'thing'—is portrayed: and thus that which is essential in the formation of a landscape, the local conditions, the situation in space, is completely left out of account. I look at a medieval illumination and perceive a man and next to him a tree. The subject demands the tree, since the man experiences something in the open air. The height of the picture-surface is about 4 inches, that of the man $3\frac{1}{4}$ inches, that of the tree $2\frac{3}{4}$ inches. The 'faulty' relation of size between the human figure and the tree is thus to be explained: the man is, to the draughtsman, that which is primary and significant, the tree, as representative of the landscape, is of secondary importance. In order to retain the 'correct' proportion of size the man would have had to be depicted small and insignificant, since the picture-space existed once and for all.

Originally every part of the picture was an independent entity, as large as the picture-space allowed, and the human being had predominance; the rest had to content themselves with such space as was left over. The real proportions of size were not considered.

10. JOACHIM PATINIR, LANDSCAPE WITH THE RIVER OF DEATH

Madrid, Prado

Example of the conception of landscape prevailing in the Netherlands about 1520

Such a habit of vision placed the greatest difficulties in the way of landscape painting. The 'thing' is finite, but to landscape belongs infinity. It is true that one could juxtapose trees, houses, rocks in a jumble, but the relation of things to the ground in the depth of space and to the source of light—in a word, to that which is essential—remained unattainable, was not considered as something to be striven for, as long as the view of the world was anthropocentric. And, moreover, in the Middle Ages too much interest was not taken in the earthly vale of tears.

In Netherlandish painting of the 15th and 16th centuries it is instructive to follow, step by step, how the landscape picture develops out of love for nature, thirst for space, and knowledge of the laws of perspective. The juxtaposition of things, with its logic of space, was first grasped by means of a gradation of the measures of size. The zones of depth are marked off from one another. The horizon is placed high, in order to make superimposition in the plane produce the effect of succession in space. Very slowly the aboriginal preference for single and complete 'things' gets overcome. Roger van der Weyden introduces trees, standing far from one another, for the vegetation of the background; Memling round bushes, which overlap in rows, yet in such a fashion that through dots of light they are distinctly set off against one another. Gerard David, who, as regards landscape, is an *auctor imperii*, sets up walls of foliage, and that in the middle distance. And finally the thicket is represented, and you no longer see the trees for the wood.

Since a tree in relation to the picture-space is excessively large, it was realized at the time when one began to notice proportions of size that everything to do with landscape was to be rendered from a considerable distance. The strong inclination to make the land clearly visible compelled the artists, however, to render the background from a near view. Giorgione's superiority to his Northern contemporaries is not least to be seen in this, that he rendered his distances from a distant view. Geographical and topographical information was demanded from the Netherlandish landscape painter. An ideal was to show the earth as a whole, with everything that is to be seen on it— an absurd task. And yet this is what Jan van Eyck, according to Facius, produced for his sovereign: *Mundi comprehensio orbiculari forma . . . quo nullum consummatius opus nostra aetate factum putatur, in quo non solum loca, situsque regionum, sed etiam locorum distantiam metiendo agnoscas.* Thus something that was half map of the world, half landscape picture, was produced. And from such landscape backgrounds as we possess by Jan van Eyck, we can form a vague idea of this missing work; we can understand also why Philip of Burgundy could entrust his painter with, and expect from him, such a performance.

While an architectural interior can be construed in conformity with the rules of perspective, it is im-

11. LUCAS CRANACH, REST ON THE FLIGHT INTO EGYPT

Berlin, Picture Gallery

1504

possible to apply rational means to landscape. The tendency of the early Netherlandish masters, and especially Roger van der Weyden, to introduce buildings into the background, and to stimulate the illusion of space, say, with streets which lead into depth—this tendency is connected with the embarrassment which these masters experienced in developing pure landscape from the point of view of perspective. Jan van Eyck, the pioneer, in whose art the old and the new clash violently, finds a way out, whenever the subject permitted it, by drawing—though not actually construing—an interior in the foreground in perspective: by concealing the middle distance: and by letting the elaborate landscape distance appear as a vista between columns, or enclosed by a window. He has done this for instance in the Rollin Madonna in the Louvre.

The custom of spreading on a surface figures, and whatever else was to be portrayed, had a long lease of life. When one had got so far as to see parts of the picture at this or that distance from the eye, one proceeded to place several picture-planes, layers, zones behind each other. In consequence the parts of landscape offer themselves as towering up, frontal and parallel to the picture-plane, just as, on the stage, landscape is created by wings, which are set up at intervals in the direction of depth on the right and the left, frontally and parallel to the dropscene. It is thus a question of a multitude of degrees, and of a stemming of the spatial tide. Only at a late stage—for the first time occasionally in Bruegel's pictures—was the primitive flatness of effect done away with.

Landscape painting became in the 16th century an independent branch of the profession. Landscape in a devotional picture was a stage, a wall in front of which the saints are standing, a vista, a background, a distance. It was still thus conceived, thus seen even after landscape painting had emancipated itself. Thirst for knowledge and respect for creation gave the youthful picture-category meaning, justification and importance. One wanted to take in the whole of the elements of landscape—mountains, trees, buildings, roads, fields, meadows, rivers—and to show anything that was to be seen on earth in its spatial connection. The principal characteristic of the world was its wideness, and in order to make it visible one ascended mountains, hills and towers. More particularly the mountain-chain, seen with the eyes of the cartographer, and striking the dweller in the lowlands as something sensational, became picture-worthy. The land had to make considerable efforts—tower up heroically, assume excitingly picturesque aspects— in order to be accepted in the first half of the 16th century as a sufficient and satisfactory content for a picture. Often a biblical or mythological motif provided an opportunity or excuse to show a glimpse of landscape. That which was primary from the point of view of content thus became secondary from the

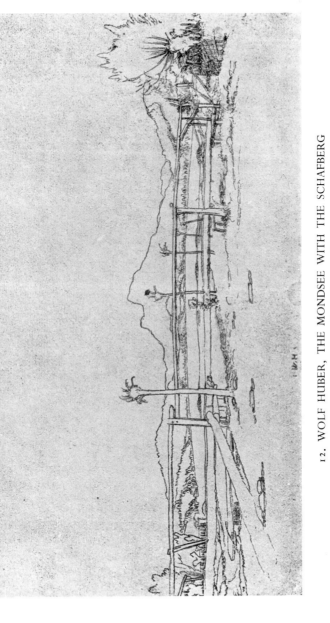

12. WOLF HUBER, THE MONDSEE WITH THE SCHAFBERG

Drawing. Nuremberg, Germanisches Museum

An early example of a simple portrayal of nature, 1510

point of view of form: it was embedded as a *staffage* and in many cases is scarcely to be discerned.

The landscape painter, from a pantheistic sense of the world, proclaimed and praised at the beginning the extent and richness of Creation; later on, its sublime and solemn quiet in contrast to petty and restless human nature.

The geographer with his love of description, the architect given to elaborate projects, the lyrical poet, all entered into conversation with the observer.

That, already at the beginning of the 16th century, one was capable of realizing unique visual experiences, notably when travelling, is proved by Dürer's water-colours, which however—and this is the decisive point—were not regarded as pictures in the full sense of the word.

If we leave out of account whether we have before us a landscape picture, strictly speaking, or a figure scene in which the landscape formations not only occupy much room, but are the bearers of the effect, then no one can deny Giorgione, the Venetian master, the distinction of being the first great landscape painter. More important in the historical context than the rapid and intermittent advances of a master of genius are the gradual advances which may be traced in the Low Countries, in the works of Jan van Eyck, Dirk Bouts, Geertgen tot Sint Jans, Jerome Bosch, Gerard David and Joachim Patinir.

Spontaneously there stirs in Southern Germany—

especially between Ratisbon and Vienna, down the Danube—independent observation of landscape. In a short space of time between 1500 and 1510, impressions of astounding directness are produced here. The schemes and conventions—referred to above and derived from tradition—whose rule we can observe in the Low Countries, appear to be powerless in Southern Germany. What we find here is more visual experience than composition, and frequently a low horizon, a forest in the middle distance, the human beings *in* the landscape, not in front of it, a love of ramification and thickets. It is not a question of a prospect, a vista, a panorama, but rather of moving and straying in nature, of mingling with nature.

Three examples may suffice to illustrate this miracle, sudden as the appearance of a meteor. Lucas Cranach's *Rest on the Flight into Egypt* in the Berlin Gallery (1504), the four panels by Rueland Frueauf the Younger in the monastery of Klosterneuburg (1507?), and the drawing by Wolf Huber in the Germanisches Museum at Nuremberg showing the Mondsee (1510). Martin Weinberger speaks, when treating of this drawing, 'of the straightforward notation of a given locality . . . . mysterious in its unaffected truthfulness'.[1] The pictures at Klosterneuburg also contain accurate transcripts of the locality. The subject—the foundation of the monastery—caused the artist to portray hills, fields and forest-land simply and with complete lack of

[1] Martin Weinberger, *Wolf Huber*, (1930), p. 30.

13. RUELAND FRUEAUF THE YOUNGER
PANEL FROM THE ALTARPIECE OF ST. LEOPOLD
Monastery of Klosterneuburg
1507?

prejudice: and, in so doing, he unrolls the smiling, springlike scene before us in a manner so independent of time that the name of Moritz von Schwind has come to the lips of many spectators. Incidentally it is said that Schwind knew these pictures well.

Cranach in his picture of 1504 provides for the Holy Family a safe resting-place in a German forest, and links up the figures indissolubly with landscape. How powerfully his imagination was haunted about this time by things growing and the life of nature is shown by his portraits—notably the marvellous pair in the Reinhart Collection at Winterthur, in which the trees with their knotty branches have penetrated into the spatial zone of the portrait-heads in the foreground.

Wilhelm Fraenger's compelling descriptions in his volume on Matthias Grünewald (1936) direct attention to the harmony between man, forest and forest retainers, a harmony which in the picture of the Hermits, the panel of the Isenheim Altarpiece, is due to the fact that the old men are approximated to the wild vegetation of the primeval forest by a kind of mimicry.

It is extraordinary how quickly this blossom was blighted. Cranach's feeling for landscape gave out completely. Altdorfer and Huber remained rather more true to themselves, but went somewhat astray —Huber into calligraphy, Altdorfer into a manner that is daintily miniature-like and favours garden-like sophistication. The venturesome advance in South-

Eastern Germany remains an episode. The main evolution is centred in the Low Countries.

Art reached an astoundingly high water mark in the
work of Jacob Ruisdael and Hobbema. Dazzled by such
superior mastery, one easily overlooks, however, how
little these masters, in any particular case, took visual
experiences as their starting-point; how restricted
was the view taken of nature as regards standpoint,
lighting, time of the year and day. Ruisdael never
wearied of rendering the melancholy peace of the
country in high summer, late in the afternoon under a
clouded sky.

An attitude of greater freedom towards nature, less
narrowed down by professional routine, was that of
the masters who occasionally painted landscapes—
above all Pieter Bruegel. He conceives landscape as a
stage set for dramatic, epic or anecdotic episodes and
human action; his follower in the 17th century is
Rubens—he, too, scarcely one of the professional
landscape painters.

A symptom of the fully matured vision of landscape
lies in the extent of the sky and its importance for the
effect of the picture. If there is something which cannot be regarded as a finite 'thing' it is aerial space,
which in consequence, to the primitive method of
vision, was empty, null and void, simply non-existent.
To the great landscape painters of the 17th century, to
a Claude, an Aelbert Cuyp, a Jacob Ruisdael, the sky
meant a great deal, and beginnings of an observation

14. LUCAS CRANACH, PORTRAIT OF JOHANN CUSPINIAN
Winterthur, Collection of Dr. O. Reinhart
1503

of the clouds and effects of light in the works of Jan van Eyck, Dirk Bouts and Altdorfer must be regarded as tentative advances.

Finally, it strikes one that the path followed by landscape painting runs parallel to the road on which painting, drawing away from sculpture, became that which it now is. It was in Haarlem and Venice, not in Florence, that landscape art blossomed forth. And the English artists, in the 18th and 19th centuries, evince much talent for landscape painting, and little indeed for sculpture.

XVIII

PORTRAITURE

THE portrait occupies a special position. Aesthetical purists have wanted to exclude it from the domain of artistic activity. Such intolerance on the part of the guardians of the temple, however, requires justification. The desire to invest the transient single case with the immortality of the picture has led to portraiture. Information as to some given facts of form is asked for. The task demands reproduction of the individual form, prosaic information, and seems to leave little scope for the will to expression. Karel van Mander tells of the Dutch academic artist Cornelis van Haarlem, that he painted wonderfully fine portraits, but unwillingly, since his spirit felt hemmed in thereby.

Within certain limits, the tendency to typify affects even portraiture. Whoever has to paint the portrait of a military leader, carries with him ideas as to the characteristics of the profession concerned, and shows us in this particular captain the 'captain as such', all the more definitely since it is desired to pay honour and confer distinction. The caricature carries that

15. LUCAS CRANACH
PORTRAIT OF THE WIFE OF JOHANN CUSPINIAN
Winterthur, Collection of Dr. O. Reinhart
1503

which is individual in another direction, but it also eventually reaches a type.

According to a charmingly ingenious myth, portrait was born as a silhouette, as the outline of a shadow.

At an early stage portrait took the form of a coin image. The small scale permitted emphasis of the typical aspect and the suppression of individual features; the profile made it possible to fix the essentials of the individual form by means of lines, as a draughtsman would. The donor, in an altarpiece or a devotional picture, also appears in a side aspect, since he turns in veneration towards a divine or holy character seen alongside of him in the picture-space. The aspect in profile secures for the personality represented, in relation to the spectator, a proud isolation, an existence in another world. The side aspect, particularly welcome to the draughtsman and the maker of reliefs, enjoyed favour for a long time.

The full face aspect is embarrassing to the draughtsman, inasmuch as in this position the boundary lines do not convey as much and as distinct information as the spaces of colour and tone. But even at a primitive stage a decision was taken in favour of the full-face aspect, from the naïve sense of need to retain everything and not to allow anything to be taken from one. We have two eyes, and a child will not reconcile itself to only one being visible.

Painting seeks to combine the advantages of both these early types by choosing the side aspect halved—

the three-quarter aspect. This turn makes it possible
to show the profile of the nose, the cheek and the fore-
head: the linear plan of the head, as it were. Both eyes
become visible. And the relation of the person represented to the spectator can be varied, since he can
turn his glance towards us or away from us. At the
same time the illusion of movement—and hence of
life—is aroused. Vision in conformity with perspective made it possible to develop this aspect, and to
favour it at the expense of the primitive form of pure
profile and pure frontality. With a special intention
—at times an archaistic one—the medal-like profile
or the decided full-face aspect have, in more or less
recent times, been chosen perhaps from a wish to
remove the person represented to a distance in the
one case, or to force his imperious presence upon the
spectator in the other. Holbein has thus immortalized
Henry VIII very effectively when seen full-face, and
Prince Edward when seen in profile—once, for that
matter, also seen full-face, an aspect which he will-
ingly chose on other occasions as well.

Individual character expresses itself in the figure
and the way of moving, not only in the face. But it
took a long time before attention was paid to the
human organism as a whole, except in the case of the
portraits of donors. The face, as it were the window
of the human body, the part which is not screened off,
seemed to suffice as an image of the personality. In the
15th and 16th centuries one may follow, step by step,

how the hands, half length, three-quarter length, full length, become picture-worthy and how the character of the person represented, his sphere of life and even momentary mood, were more and more expressed in his gesture and attitude. The full-length, life-size portrait was exceptionally developed already by Bernhard Strigel (about 1510), and by Holbein; definitely later by Titian, Giambattista Moroni, Antonio Moro and Nicholas Neufchatel. Jan van Eyck's double portrait of Arnolfini and his wife is in its period something unique.

In order to understand the development of portraiture one must realize that, in the distant past, it was pre-eminently sovereigns that were depicted, and that this was done in the spirit of setting up a monument to them. A reverent gaze upwards fixed the features of the great for the benefit of posterity. In the Middle Ages, the figures of donors were treated as portraits. A personality was thus in those days portrayed in passive or active connection with veneration. That which is individual asserted itself slowly and gradually against ritual or courtly convention. First man, then woman, finally the child were realized in their individual and concrete selves. Since the painter was a man, and the social position of woman was not a free one, the feminine face was more or less decisively moulded upon an ideal of beauty. In the double portrait by Jan van Eyck, Arnolfini has much more individuality than his wife.

127

Among Memling's portraits there are many halves of diptychs, with the sitter's hands joined in prayer and turned towards the Madonna. The single portraits by the master, which did not come into being as parts of devotional pictures, hardly differ in conception and expression from the portraits of donors, so that in this respect the influence of an ecclesiastical spirit upon portraiture still makes itself felt towards the end of the 15th century.

The self-portrait provides the psychologist with an opportunity for stimulating speculation. Externally it may be recognized through the glance directed decisively at the spectator—since the painter looked at himself in a mirror, and the attention, seemingly addressed to us, was devoted to his own appearance. This entails a self-revelation, an emergence from the picture to a degree which usually is not characteristic of portraits. Man does not take up a neutral or objective attitude towards his own appearance; his participation is coloured more by his 'will' than by his 'idea'. Self-portraits do not confirm the view that we know ourselves better than others. They are not in a particularly high degree 'good likenesses'. Observation is interfered with by vanity, by ambition. The painter wants to cut a figure; he takes himself overseriously, portrays himself in a definite situation, namely, as gazing, with open eyes, in tension and action. The ordinary sitter on the other hand, the person whose portrait is being painted, gets tired and

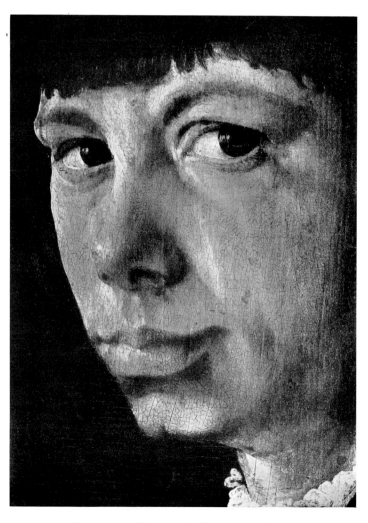

16. LUCAS VAN LEYDEN, PORTRAIT OF THE ARTIST
Detail. Brunswick, Museum
about 1510

bored. For this reason self-portraits are aggressive and dramatic, and not infrequently theatrical. They convey to us less what the painter looked like than what he wanted to look like. One may speak of a rhetoric of the self-portrait.

The ideal portrait—that is, the likeness of a personality never seen by the artist—was a task with which the painter often used to be confronted. Every saint was an individual being. The medieval painter hardly felt the contradiction implied by his task, all the more so as the perishable earthly body did not claim much attention. A vague pictorial tradition, a longer or shorter beard, and mainly the emblems sufficed to make the saints recognizable. Only when heightened illusion of life and, consequently, a portrait-like appearance was demanded, did the artists find themselves faced with the difficult and complicated duty of establishing a harmony between their knowledge of a personality and a chosen model—and at times, moreover, a more or less binding pictorial tradition. An important illustration of the manner in which a Netherlandish painter of the 15th century dealt with the problem is provided by the series of famous intellectuals in the Ducal Palace at Urbino, painted by Justus of Ghent. The grandest example, however, the monumental solution of the problem, is provided in Dürer's picture known as the *Four Apostles*. With deep earnestness the German artist strove fo didactic effect beyond the feeble pictorial tradition and that which was available in the models: he perceived the four witnesses of faith as representatives of the temperaments, and forced thereby that which was chance and accident into a system. What he achieved by high tension of imagination is appearance full of vitality, but also types; a self-contained whole, since according to the ideas of the time there only existed four temperaments; moreover, powerful contrasts, and, finally, the impression that these men, however different from one another, are united in one exhortation, one warning, one message, one faith. Portrait and Idea are here married to one another; the ideal portrait in the highest sense has been achieved.

17. HANS MEMLING, STILL LIFE
Lugano, Castle Rohoncz Collection
on the reverse of the Portrait, reproduced Plate 1

XIX

STILL LIFE

STILL life, too, had its germ in the devotional picture. Notably the Northern masters did not resist the inclination to turn their attention to 'dead' objects, long before this picture category had emancipated itself. In the 17th and 18th centuries fruit, flowers and objects of every kind were depicted everywhere, often, however, in a decorative context and by painters whose talent was held in relatively low esteem. Almost exclusively in the Low Countries did one look upon a vase of flowers, a table laden with food, as a wholly valid subject for a self-contained easel picture.

In Holland the 17th century was the period of the rise of the middle class. The youthful delight in 'good things'—in wine, fruit, fish, lobsters—was stimulated in front of pictures. A prince, who is accustomed to have delicious food placed before him, does not attach so much importance to these products as the burgher who has got on in the world, or may hope to get on. The quantity, the superb and magnificent ripeness, of nourishing things glorify the bliss of the earth. Kalf proclaims luxury tempered with taste. In Antwerp an overwhelming mass of welcome goods is accumulated Baroque-fashion—say by Snyders and Jan Fyt—while in Holland exquisite things are arranged, as by Kalf and van Beyeren. In the former case it is the *gourmand*, in the latter the *gourmet* who is catered for. In the healthy delight in life, which irradiates from the Netherlandish still life, the Italian and Spanish painters of such subjects have scarcely any share.

In the devotional pictures of the 15th century the details of furniture—especially in the cosy habitation of the Virgin—were carried out most lovingly, also, as a symbolic addition, such things as the vessel containing a lily in renderings of the Annunciation. One of the most beautiful portraits by Memling, which from Scottish ownership has found its way to the Rohoncz collection at Lugano, shows on the reverse, as a decorative, perhaps also symbolic, afterthought, a table with a Persian rug on which stands an Italian vessel filled with flowers.

The meat-counters and market-stalls, which Pieter Aertsen unhesitatingly about 1550 placed in the foreground of Biblical scenes, represent early stages of the Flemish fruit pieces, as Snyders and Fyt painted them in the 17th century. The *Vanitas* still life, with books, originated in the pictures of St. Jerome, in which we see the Saint meditating in his study. Presumably a picture by Jan van Eyck in the possession of the Me-

18. MARINUS VAN REYMERSWAELE, ST. JEROME IN HIS STUDY

Madrid, Prado

Origin of the Vanitas Still Life

dici and now lost was the source from which Petrus
Christus drew, in his picture at Detroit; and it even
influenced Ghirlandaio in his fresco in the church of
the Ognissanti at Florence. Moreover, in the altarpiece by Jan van Eyck which belonged to Alfonso,
King of Naples, St. Jerome was represented in his
study, and the Italians marvelled here also at the still
life of books. In the 16th century Marinus van Reymerswaele often painted the saintly scholar and in so
doing always alluded to the transitoriness of the things
of this world by means of a mass of dry and desiccated
things, such as written-on parchments and a skull.
Still life has, as a symbol, proclaimed growing and
flowering just as much as passing and dying.

No people and no period have represented everything visible with so uniform and loving a sympathy
as the Dutch of the 17th century; with so objective,
almost scientific, an accuracy of perception; without
asking about the spiritual significance and valuing the
things accordingly. They could as it were copy from
nature grapes, or the skin of a dead hare, without in-
curring any risk, seeing that a single apple perfectly
represents the category, or 'idea', of the apple.

Woe to the master who looks at the human face
with the eye of the still-life painter!

XX

THE ARTIST: GENIUS AND TALENT

FORMERLY pictures and sculptures were produced in the same spirit as furniture; that is to say, the professional attitude, the relation of the producer to his patron or client, and his social position were those of the craftsman. Art separated in recent times from craftsmanship, or rather, craftsmanship and art parted company—to the disadvantage not only of craftsmanship. Punctuality of delivery, fulfilment of the agreed conditions, solidity of execution were in past days demanded from painters and sculptors, and remuneration adjusted to the time spent. Even Dürer, on asking for a higher honorarium from a Frankfurt patron, still refers not to his name or the superiority of his artistic performance, but to the unexpectedly heavy claim upon his time, and to the high cost of the colours employed. The sons of painters became painters: in choosing a trade one did not wait for special gifts to announce themselves.

We link with the concept 'artist' ideas of special qualifications of selectedness, of rare gifts, of an ability which is not gained by industry and practice. The activity of the artist appears uncontrollable and does not fit into the general order of useful, necessary and profitable labour. The craftsman is more deeply indebted to society, to the community, than the artist, and in a different way. The admiration which comes the way of the artist has an admixture of suspicion. His position depends on fame, and fame on the uncertain, changeable artistic judgment. Youth lives on the hope for recognition, old age on the prestige gained by performance—or else on defiant contempt of public opinion and expectation of posthumous fame. The duty towards himself, to which the artist appeals so proudly, is strictly speaking nothing less than a duty.

The 'great name', which compensates the artist for the loss of social security, becomes only with the 15th century once again accessible to painters and sculptors. The thought that a master of classical Greece was able to keep his fame unobscured all through the dark ages probably fired the spirits of the 15th century, heightened the general esteem of the artist's profession, and stimulated ambition to great deeds.

Already about 1400 the Limburg *Chronicle* speaks of a painter named Wilhelm 'who, according to the judgment of the Masters, had been the best in the German lands'. Here we thus already find an order of precedence, the bold superlative of appreciation. It still took, however, a long time before social position was determined through the recognition of uncommon gifts. To begin with, in the 15th century some masters, who had freed themselves from the restrictions of the Guild organization, managed to get absorbed among the crowd of Court retainers—the jesters, the mistresses, the adulatory poets.

In the 16th century painters and sculptors, striving to rank with the intellectual workers, associated themselves with the scholars and thinkers—Leonardo and Dürer are cases in point. In the practice of craftsmanship, conception and execution were indissolubly linked together. The dualistic idea, which in the 16th century crops up in the inscriptions '*invenit et fecit*', points to a pride which separates spiritual ownership from manual labour and claims the former for itself.

The 17th century witnessed the painter-prince, a type which Rubens embodies most perfectly. His financial success, his social rise, were at any rate partly due to his artistic powers. But it must be recognized that qualities of his character, intellectual gifts, the manner of a man of the world, diplomatic ability, all contributed to the result. A reflection of this light fell on the English portrait painters of the 18th century and still upon some painters of the 19th century like Makart or Lenbach; painters who enjoyed their posthumous fame while still alive, and consumed it.

In the 19th century the concept 'artist' became sharply determined. To quote Goethe:

> *The song that rises from the throat*
> *Repays the minstrel well*

—that is a typical Romantic idea.

BOHEMIANISM

Outside, and at times above, *bourgeois* society, running the risk of a financial decline, free and beyond the law, the artist despised the 'philistine' and created for himself a social class, with special renunciations and special pretensions. Bohemianism blossomed forth when Romanticism turned into the taverns and cafés of the great cities.

A posthumous fame has above all come the way of those painters of the 19th century who belonged neither to the type of the painter-prince nor to that of the Bohemian, but who, on the contrary, in austere and untiring industry, led a middle-class life, and even felt some yearning for the solidity of handicraft.

The process of transformation here sketched—memorable in the history of civilization—modified the nature of production. The intensified striving after fame carried nervous tension, jealousy, and a desire to attract attention into the workshops. One was accustomed to go to market in order to buy things which were good value and were useful; one goes to exhibitions in order to experience thrills and discover talent. A shrill note, a wilful emphasis and over-accentuation of individuality, the extravagant instead of the extraordinary—these become doubtful features on the surface of up-to-date production. Only authentic gifts, firmly self-contained, could hold out in this mad confusion.

The style of a period changes in reciprocal contact with fashion, which moves on a lower plane. While fashion, prescribing dress and coiffure, rushes forward fleet of foot, that taste which determines artistic production advances rather with circumspection, conditioned by a necessity which is deeply rooted. Fashion in recent times, baited by economic interests, has assumed a whirlwind tempo; and it has infected artistic production.

Refined taste alongside of slight gifts—a combination which nowadays is not exactly rare—must entail that the painter feels that the things which he sees are commonplace, and thereupon tries passionately to invent something that he has not seen. Thus are born manners of art, not very differently from fashions of dress. Since it has been successfully conveyed to the public that it must praise what displeases it, the public agrees to everything.

The craftsman became an artist, but he also became a scholar or a manufacturer, a contractor or a virtuoso. The relation of virtuoso to artist is that of manner to style. The expression, originally meant as praise of exceptional ability, contains in our terminology a connotation which is not devoid of reservation, doubt and caution. A consciously developed skill, an exhibition of one's ability in an endeavour to please, that is what we call virtuosity, in contrast to naïvely original power of creation. Most frequently the expression is used, without a derogatory implication, of reproductive musicians.

That the artist tells us his name and assumes responsibility for his performance through his signature, is nowadays the general custom. This developed gradually in connection with the awakening and intensification of the consciousness of one's own worth. It is no accident that great masters like Giotto, Simone Martini, and Jan van Eyck should call out their names in times when this was by no means the general custom. This habit spread curiously and unevenly. As late as the 17th or 18th centuries many painters either did not sign at all, or did so only exceptionally—Rubens, Van Dyck and Watteau, for instance. Here it was customary to sign, there not. Rules cannot be formulated, psychological explanations are unavailable. As a trade mark, as a protection against copying, the signature was fairly regularly employed in engraving and woodcut. Precisely those masters who also produced woodcuts and engravings—such as Dürer, Lucas van Leyden and Jacob Cornelisz.—have signed their paintings too; if not always, yet frequently.

A place entirely apart is occupied by the celebrated lines on the Ghent altarpiece. Prolix, laudatory, rhetorical, like the inscription on a monument, they are hardly conceivable as the utterance of a painter in the first half of the 15th century, and are therefore suspect, apart from other arguments which have been produced against them.

The artist with his inner struggles and tragic conflicts, not understood by the dull crowd, has in the 19th century become the subject and the hero of high-flying poetical treatment. The conception was heightened into something mystical. The painters are hard put to it to correspond to the expectations which an imagination, fed on novels, entertains with regard to them. In consequence there followed inevitably disappointment on one side, the pose of 'genius' on the other. The artist who, in the popular view, only has the choice between being a genius or nothing, looks like a 'sick eagle'. The phrase was coined by Hugo von Hofmannsthal.

To draw the boundary line between genius and talent has never been done quite successfully, though attempts are continuously being made. If one thinks of a difference of degree, then it would surely be difficult to indicate a point on the scale where genius begins. A generally valid indication of the contrast is probably not to be found.

Michelangelo, Grünewald, Rembrandt are unhesitatingly described as masters of genius: indeed, to apply the concept of 'talent' to these creative personalities would be inappropriate and almost sound like blasphemy. A performance which exceeds expectation, prevision and estimate; sharp-edged individuality; defiant opposition to compromise; an attitude of 'this cannot be otherwise'; a spiritual obsession, which is akin to madness—these are somewhat obvious characteristics of the genius, which operates outside the conventions of taste of its period, in tragic isolation. We speak of a *melancholia ingenii* and think of mental struggles against inner and outer resistance. Genius seems to evince itself in will rather than in achievement, in conquest rather than in rule.

We extend to talented artists our appreciation and sympathy, feeling that in their praiseworthy activity they nevertheless remain on our level. Their vision is familiar to us, it contains indeed more and better things, but not anything fundamentally different from our own vision. They occupy a height which can be scaled. Of Rembrandt and Frans Hals it has been said, subtly and appositely, that in front of works by the latter one is seized by a wish to paint, and before works by the former one loses any such wish. Thereby a difference, which I have tried to define, is perhaps not badly indicated, and the incomprehensibleness and unapproachableness, which are peculiar to a creation of genius, fixed within their limits.

Among the greatest masters to whom the title of genius is commonly not denied, there are happy and harmonious natures to which my definition does not seem to apply; who stand before us not as fighters but as victors. On the other hand we find artists who do not incontestably belong to the category of the greatest and nevertheless, through their boldness of imagination and strongly marked individuality, claim the title of genius—Greco, Van Gogh or Böcklin, for instance. Now and then we feel indeed an inclination to say: a genius, but not a talent. In this way a difference of kind between genius and talent outlines itself perhaps most clearly. The concept of genius indicates a closer alliance to the spiritual than to the visual. Grillparzer has said: 'Only from the union of character with talent issues that which is called genius.' However, one can probably find elsewhere other, more convincing definitions. But the union of specific gifts to greatness of soul and strength of spirit may be peculiar to genius.

XXI

ART AND ERUDITION

ERUDITION has turned to art late, has perhaps hesitated to do so from an expectation that this union would not be productive of many blessings. The scholar, who concerns himself with art, generally clasps emptiness. He woos the capricious beauty, now in this fashion, now in that, and as a result succeeds in seizing the garment rather than the body. He experiments as historian, as philologist or as a scientist. He is a philologist inasmuch as he examines literary accounts critically, an epigraphist when he investigates inscriptions, a scientist when he examines works of art with a view to deriving chemical and physical information from them. Naturally he is compelled, by such many-sided activity, to seek help from others and to read a tremendous lot. The excessive black-and-white diet is not wholesome to his eyes. Since we live in the age of the scientific disciplines, whose methods enjoy an almost superstitious veneration, he is particularly fond of keeping company with the scientists. He lives in a continuous fear of losing dignity through his contact with something as slight as art, and of not being admitted to the circle of the serious and re-spected University dons.

History, whatever its subject, is in a difficult posi-tion among the scholarly disciplines. Frequently enough people have refused to acknowledge its true scientific character. Art history has apparently an ad-vantage over other branches of history; it claims superiority with some justification, especially over political history. The works of art are there before our eyes, as it were, as a preserved 'spirit of the times'. Only, let us not forget the words of Goethe:

> *What Spirit of the Times you call*
> *Good Sirs, is but your spirit after all*
> *In which the times are seen reflected.*

Nevertheless, something survives that mirrors itself, while the historian, so far as politics are concerned, is thrown back exclusively upon literary tradition, and distils his truth—mostly, not entirely without a political tendency—out of a hundred inaccurate, if not definitely mendacious, and mutually contradictory reports. The deeds of the artists we can perceive for ourselves; of the deeds of the kings an echo reaches us—we hear mostly what the victors have let their scribes put down.

The image is older than writing, and for long stretches of time the sole provider of information and evidence.

Now it should be remembered that works of art do

not speak—they sing, and can therefore only be understood by listeners upon whom the Muses have bestowed their gifts.

Grillparzer expresses himself somewhere approximately thus: 'Whoever writes a history of chemistry, must be a chemist, and can only as a chemist become a historian.' I wonder if this does not apply to art history? And Schiller says: 'There exists only one vessel for the reception of works of imagination, namely, imagination'.

Since artistic activity, whatever else it may be, is in every case a process of emotionally spiritual nature, the science of art is bound to be psychology. It may also be something else, but it is psychology in all circumstances. Since, however, all psychology depends upon experience of what has happened to oneself spiritually and emotionally, it follows that only an artistically gifted spectator can penetrate into the nature of artistic production. We approach thereby the deduction that only the practising artist is entitled to judge. This deduction is erroneous.

The productive artist is incapable of assuming, with regard to his own work and the work of others, the receptive, observing attitude from which enlightenment may be expected. He produces naïvely and unconsciously; his experiences lie too deep for it to be possible for him to bring them to the light. Accordingly, his confessions in letters, autobiographies or theoretical expositions are valuable only as indirect evidence—as such they possess, however, great value: but they must be subjected to interpretation. The producing artist cannot be accepted as a judge, since he cannot free himself from his own artistic formula, which is tied from the point of view of time, place and individuality; and he is the less capable of doing this, in the measure that his own gifts are original, fertile and thirsting for expression. And, after all, he has other and better things to do than to indulge in philosophizing; and he may even have a presentiment that knowledge does away with ability to produce, or at any rate weakens it—something that is noticeable in the individual development of many artists in civilized ages. And yet there is more to be learnt from the stammering utterances of artists than from the well-constructed, systematic treatises of the aestheticians.

In front of art the thinkers are mostly blind, and the practising artists mostly dumb. There only remains the artistically gifted, but non-productive, spectator as the one who is capable of insight and deeper understanding, and called upon to provide enlightenment.

Artistic production and contemplation of art are activities which have more in common with one another than is usually assumed. The creative imagination stands in the same relationship to the receptive as the cog-wheel to the cog-rail. The lover of art shares with the creative artist an abnormally sensitive receptiveness. His emotional life reacts quickly and violently to optical signals. The ability to produce, the capacity to realize vision are absent in him, whether it be that his interior images are not distinct enough, or that his hand lacks skill. His is a platonic talent, so to speak, even a 'Raphael without hands'. He possesses a reliable memory for visual experiences, and indeed not because he has, shall we say, eagerly learnt things by heart, but because—extending his emotional sympathy, and living in a state of excitement which softens the wax of the tablets of memory —he has experienced delight in contemplation. Form and colour are retained in his memory for decades; not in the sense, it is true, that he would be able to produce, reproduce or even describe them, but certainly in the sense that an appearance, presenting itself once again, is recognized by him and greeted as something familiar. Emotion and the senses have a much better memory than the intellect.

It can be contested that there exists a science of art; at least the concept 'science' can be defined so narrowly that art as a subject accessible to her is eliminated.

Every scientific effort presupposes a terminology which covers the field of knowledge concerned, and through which the scholar can convey to other scholars his reasons, deductions and conclusions in an unambiguous manner. Even the greatest optimist will not maintain that art criticism can comply with this demand. If I judge a work of art, and employ words in order to give reasons for my opinion, I am far removed from thinking that I have expressed with those words that which has caused my judgment. The modifications, blendings and shades in emotional life, which truly determined my opinion, are not to be seized with verbal pincers.

An honest striving after knowledge may be recognized as science, even here, where the results remain questionable, and do not make themselves plain to reason.

Science, in conformity with its nature, is striving for the goal of establishing necessity; it hates accident. It must not rest content with establishing: 'this is the case'; rather, it must prove, 'this is the case for such and such a reason'. The historian comes, however, everywhere upon accident, while he does not notice necessity—which yet is his constant concern—but invents and imagines it. That Rubens and Van Dyck both worked in Antwerp at the same time, that Schongauer had died by the time that Dürer went to Colmar in search of him, these are accidents in the sense in which one may at all speak of accident; and that such accidents have had a share in determining the development of artistic production is not to be denied. In order to avoid coming up against accident, one has set up the ideal of a 'history of art without names', being moved by the desire to recognize a course of events which is governed by law, and which takes

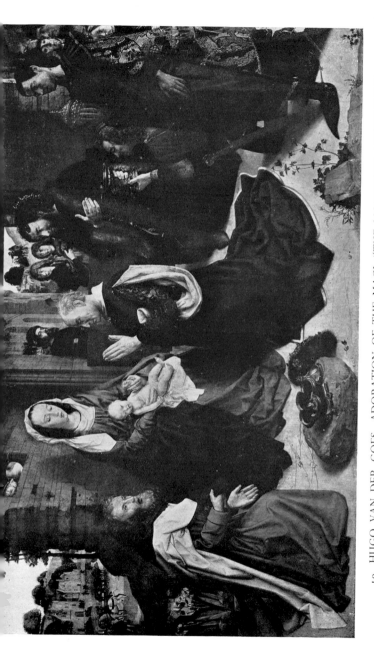

19. HUGO VAN DER GOES, ADORATION OF THE MAGI ('THE MONFORTE ALTARPIECE')

Berlin, Picture Gallery

place independently of the intervention of individual artists here and there, now and then.

I will leave undecided the old question, debated by philosophers concerned with history, as to the greater or smaller effect exercised upon the course of events by heroes who 'accidentally' have emerged at a given time and in a given place. In any case, even if I aim at a 'history of art without names', I am yet bound to have classified the works of art according to time and place, and as far as possible to have brought them into harmony with biographical tradition, before I attempt to say something about the general development of the will for art. To someone who knows nothing about Correggio's life, it might happen that he would assign the works of this master to the 17th century, and in no case would he be able to classify them as, in their essence, affording evidence regarding Parma and the time about 1520. When the Monforte altarpiece by Hugo van der Goes arrived at Berlin, a sensitive art historian—to whom 'history of art without names' was a desirable goal—terrified me by his remark that the picture obviously was a work of the 16th century, and hence could not possibly be by Hugo van der Goes, who, of course, died in the 15th century.

The boundaries of the style of a given period may only be drawn, it is claimed, after all that was produced had been examined. And when would this be?

To the art historian there is available evidence of a

twofold kind. On the one hand we have tradition as contained in writings, posthumous fame, records, inventories, biographies; and on the other, the surviving works. The task consists in building bridges from one bank to the other, in bringing the documents into harmony with the surviving examples. Were all the works by Raphael lost, we would nevertheless, thanks to the utterances of his contemporaries, have an idea of his importance, his influence and even of his manner of art. Since we have a considerable part of his life's work before our eyes, we enrich and vary that idea as a result of contemplation. It becomes the task of style criticism to 'attribute' the works, to classify them according to time and place, and to fit them into the frame of tradition represented by art literature and records.

The community of art scholars consists of two groups—one may even say, two parties. The university chairs are mostly occupied by people who like to call themselves historians, and in the museum offices you meet the 'experts'. The historians strive generally from the general to the particular, from the abstract to the concrete, from the intellectual to the visible. The experts move in the opposite direction, and both mostly never get further than half-way—incidentally, without meeting each other.

The ideal set up by the historians is called 'history of the spirit'. It seems indeed most desirable that all visible results of artistic activity be considered as expressions of the continuously changing spiritual forces of humanity, in connection with other expressions to be found say in politics, literature, manners and customs, and economics. It seems perfectly possible that the experts—thus, people who take the individual work of art as their starting-point—through fixing their aim high may approach that exalted goal; and it is certainly to be desired that they and the historians should join forces. When one passes from theory to practice there is, however, lack of mutual confidence. The historians look down upon the pettifogging fuss with detail of the 'experts', who, for their part, accuse their colleagues at the universities of facing the works of art with prejudiced views. Both reproaches are justified.

On the defects peculiar to connoisseurship—spiritual narrowness, subjectivity questionable from the scientific point of view, an inclination to be guided by sentiment, also uncertainty—I shall yet have to speak, from abundant experience. As regards the performance of the historians, however, I may illustrate straightaway the dangers connected with their activities.

An aspiring scholar, intending to show himself worthy of university honours, plans a book on 'Art during the Period of the Counter-Reformation'. By assiduous reading he informs himself about the political, religious and philosophical aspects of the movement and acquires an idea of some of the features characteristic of the spiritual life of the period. He then turns to the works of art, and in them finds proof and confirmatory evidence of his conception of the spirit of the period, gained by reading. Thanks to the quantity and variety of the buildings, sculptures and paintings, dating from the time, there is much that can be found. And he who seeks, and knows from the start what he is going to find, cannot possibly go wrong. Moreover it is in the nature of a work of art to speak ambiguously, like an oracle.

The freshness of observation, the capacity for an unprejudiced reception of artistic impressions, may well be endangered through such efforts.

If the scholar takes the concept of 'the Baroque' as his starting-point he will feel inclined to fit all forces stirring in the 17th century into a scheme, and this cannot be done without applying violence. Even Rembrandt is forced into the bed of Procrustes. To be sure the searching eye, guided by a knowledge of history, can bring hidden things to light, but the mobility, receptiveness and lack of prejudice of the contemplation of art are as a result narrowed down and suffer grievously. Blindness to everything that slips through the wide meshes of the hunting net of expectations, is inevitable.

The expert is at pains to complete and differentiate the materials for study; the historian has little interest in the increase of the works of art which he has to consider, particularly as he draws his conclusions much more easily from ten than from a hundred pieces of evidence. One can perfectly well write an excellent book on Raphael by exclusively noticing the narrow circle of absolutely certain works, and without attempting to effect additions by means of style criticism, paying more heed to the purity than to the completeness of the entire picture. But the clearer the notion at which the biographer arrives, the more forcibly is it going to act as a magnet, which attracts some examples out of the troubled mass of questionable works. Whoever knows something, does also recognize it, and whoever does not recognize, reveals thereby that he does not know. The historian becomes, whether he wants it or not, an expert. Throughout the literature of art history it can be traced, how scarcely anyone of the scholars, inclined towards the history of the spirit, has on principle evaded determination of authorship. And, in view of the performance of Carl Justi it is permissible to express the hope that the difference between historian and expert may be bridged over.

A fundamental evil from which art-historical erudition suffers, seems to me to spring from the method which, put to good use in other disciplines, has mistakenly been associated with the contemplation of art. Art history, which is frequently described as young, or even as still in the nursery, appears to the typical university mind as a playful child in need of education, who must first of all learn seriousness from the grown-up branches of learning. I remember a very learned colleague once saying: 'Unfortunately I have no time, being busily engaged on other important work; otherwise I would take up the Hubert and Jan van Eyck question and settle it.' Such optimistic determination may, in other domains, be conducive to untiring, systematic and fertile performance; with regard to art, it proves a complete failure. The method which we employ—if indeed the word method be here applicable—must be won from the object; that is, irrational art. One should look at works of art without any intention of deriving knowledge, and rejoice if sometimes, as of itself, a confirmation or enrichment of our knowledge comes in a flash; and one should not approach them with the determination to solve a problem. One must let them speak, one must converse with them, but one must not interrogate them. To an inquisitor they refuse any information.

A continuity of knowledge, such as elsewhere fertilizes the whole of scientific discipline, is almost completely unavailing with regard to art. It is true that art historians read a lot, copy or assert the reverse of that which they have read—which is not much more difficult than to copy—but if one enquires by whom and in what manner our knowledge has been enriched, one usually comes upon the lover of art who, independently of predecessors, has naïvely faced the works of art. Everyone must here start scratch and be able to forget what he has read.

XXII

THE STANDPOINT OF THE SPECTATOR

IF I look at a work of art of the 15th century, I am incapable of eliminating what I have perceived in works of later date, and must inevitably judge from the standpoint of my own time. Any attempt to avoid this 'injustice' could at best be made by a dry-as-dust spectator, whose 'just' appreciations would be worthless. If we concern ourselves intensely with the art of the past, we acquire some practice in displacing our standpoint and in being more or less mobile in adopting now this, now that, standard. The art historian resembles at times the traveller who has been everywhere, is knowledgeable wherever he goes, but is nowhere at home. The fixed and inalienable point to which we always return, is and remains our home in time and space.

Every age receives fresh eyes. The Italian sees things differently from the German. I see differently from you, see differently to-day from yesterday. From this one might deduce that the art of days that are gone is strange, dead, incomprehensible and in-accessible to us. And this is the case in a higher

degree than is usually admitted. The historian, so to
speak, corrects his natural sight—as well as may be
—through spiritual spectacles; from affectation the
layman pretends familiarity, where shyness and un-
easiness predominate. He who would be able to expose the real feelings of museum visitors, would
acquire a terrifying idea of the ineffectualness of
ancient art.

Everyone begins by understanding and enjoying the
production of his own time. At least, this is the
healthy, normal and natural start. Our respect for
celebrity causes us then to rise to an understanding
of the old masters. More than one collector has ap-
proached Primitive art in stages. Adolf Thiem for instance, a gifted and independent lover of art, bought
pictures by Menzel and Daubigny when he was forty:
by Van Dyck, when he was sixty: by Memling and
Dirk Bouts when he was seventy. And many collectors have travelled in the same direction.

The sense of strangeness with regard to the work
of past ages—a sense which even the most assiduous
historian never quite overcomes—is to this extent an
advantage, that a certain distance makes us observe
that which is characteristic of time and place more
distinctly than he who is close up. When we arrive in
China we are, it is true, unable to tell one Chinaman
from another, but that which is Chinese is all the
clearer in our eyes. Without any question, the work
of Botticelli seemed to the contemporaries of the

master more natural and less severely stylized than to us. One can raise, but not answer, the question whether this has brought about an increase or decrease of artistic value.

We change the standards and thereby arrive at results which are different from one another. All comparisons may become fertile and instructive. One may compare Jan van Eyck with Roger van der Weyden, or with Manet. In every case it is useful to arrive at clearness as to the standard which has been applied.

A demand is often made—with an intention to instruct, and seeming to proclaim highest justice—that every artist is to be measured by applying to him his own standards; but this demand, strictly speaking, argues thoughtlessness. It is as if one were to measure a yard with a yard.

The historian considers it as a duty of neutrality to extend sympathy to every expression of art, and up to a point he succeeds in this. He should, however, at no time forget that a universal receptiveness, carried to an extreme, leads to aesthetic Nihilism—and, indeed, a decadence of taste among the learned scribes can frequently be observed.

In surveying artistic activity from one point of vantage—namely, our home in time and space—we gain a general picture which, it is true, is distorted in point of perspective, but homogeneous.

Each generation chooses its favourite from amongst the succession of old Masters, in conformity with its

method of vision and its own production, always inclined boldly to contradict the previous generation.
Enthronement does not take place without a tumult
and not without making the seat free by deposing
someone else. Böcklin has thus been deposed in
favour of Manet, and Velazquez in favour of Greco.
With the passing of time the exaggerations of excited
propagandists are smoothed down. But we never re-
vert to the opinions of our fathers and ancestors.

Drastic instruction regarding the change of taste is
obtainable by throwing a comparative glance at prices
paid for pictures at sales by auction. In the year 1850,
at the sale of the property left by the late King William II of Holland—a sale which spelt fatality for Holland as a collecting country—the following prices
were realized.

Jan van Eyck, *The Annunciation*	fl. 5375
(now National Gallery, Washington)	
Jan van Eyck, *The Lucca Madonna*	fl. 3000
(now Staedel Museum, Frankfurt)	
Jan Both, *Italian Landscape*	fl. 10,400
Jacob Ruisdael, *Landscape*	fl. 12,900
Hobbema, *Landscape*	fl. 27,000
Andrea del Sarto	fl. 30,350
Leonardo da Vinci	fl. 40,000
Jean Kobell	fl. 4900
Koekkoek	fl. 3500
Carlo Dolci	fl. 5900

These are particularly startling examples. A Koek-koek brought more than the *Lucca Madonna* by Jan van Eyck.

Within a generation judgment varies, but not in the degree that can be expected from the comparison of written and oral utterances. Rembrandt is greater than Gerard Dou, Jan van Eyck greater than Carlo Dolci. Nobody will to-day contradict such a statement; only everyone will feel shy of making it. The wide domain of banality is also the domain of that which has general validity.

XXIII

ON THE VALUE OF THE DETERMINATION OF
AUTHORSHIP

IF the determination of the authorship of an individual work of art most certainly is not the ultimate and highest task of artistic erudition; even if it
were no path to the goal: nevertheless, without a
doubt, it is a school for the eye, since there is no for-
mulation of a question which forces us to penetrate so
deeply into the essence of the individual work as that
concerning the identity of the author. The individual
work, rightly understood, teaches us what a compre-
hensive knowledge of universal artistic activity is incapable of teaching us.

Goethe's works were published under his name;
nothing is attributed to him or declared not to be by
him. One might imagine that the understanding of
Goethe's language, spiritual nature and development
would be greater than it is, if scribes would have had
gradually to put together his *œuvre*. They would
scarcely have performed their task with complete success, but they would have learnt a good deal as a result of their efforts.

Over long stretches of time the determination of authorship seems to be impossible. Many productions, notably of architecture, can be fixed in time—in the case of architecture the localization is always, and in the case of sculpture often, available—but they are not recognized as the expressions of individual talents. Anonymity is a symptom of deficient knowledge, even if the deficiency often is inevitable. Strictly speaking, every work of man is the product of a personality with qualities, existing once and unique. Whoever arrives in China, thinks at first that all Chinamen look alike; it is only gradually that he learns to distinguish individualities. A similar experience is that of the connoisseur who approaches the 'dark' periods. Admittedly a personality reveals itself according to the period more or less definitely in its activity. The ultimate, the most fruitful question, even if it cannot be answered, is and remains that which concerns personality.

Fairly frequently one hears the plausible-sounding objection that we know that there were hundreds of painters, yet all the existing works are divided up amongst comparatively few names. A statistical computation may serve as a defence against these misgivings. It is chiefly the prominent works that have survived, and of the surviving ones it is again the best ones that are collected, exhibited in museums and accessible to art lovers. Finally, I possess hundreds and hundreds of photographs of Netherlandish pictures of the 15th and 16th centuries which I cannot attribute, of which scarcely two seem to be by the same hand. These nameless pieces mostly are value-less and devoid of character. From this I think one may conclude that the many painters who are un-known to us have mainly produced unimportant things; and that, on the other hand, the better work with which the determination of authorship concern-itself are due to relatively few artists. This calcu-lation applies to Netherlandish and German painting of the 15th and 16th centuries; it may not be valid, or is perhaps valid in a lesser degree, for other countries and other periods.

XXIV

ON THE OBJECTIVE CRITERIA OF
AUTHORSHIP

SINCE the expert, especially when he assumes the part of the didactic writer, experiences the difficulty or impossibility of convincing others of the truth of his verdicts, he attaches great importance to objective characteristics. Just as a tired swimmer breathing a sigh of relief welcomes firm ground under his feet, so does the expert react to inscriptions, documents and objective data of different kinds. Without being able to swim he would, to be sure, not have been able to reach land: on long distances the water is so deep that it is necessary to swim.

I class among objective criteria:

1. Signatures and monograms, which give or hint at the name of the master.
2. Documentary information, agreements, inventories, catalogues which are approximately coeval with the works of art described in them; also the references to existing works in early writings, for instance the *Lives* of Vasari and Karel van Mander.
3. Measurably similar forms which, familiar to us from authenticated, signed or recognized works,

reappear in those to be attributed, say in the architecture or ornament. Under this heading is to be introduced the similarity of form of the ear, the hand, the finger nail, so strongly emphasized by Morelli.

As regards the signatures, it is to be noted that their evidence may be misleading. The name may have been added later, *bona fide* or *mala fide*, the genuine may have been removed and replaced by a forged one. A test with spirits—which are resisted by the original layer of colour—has not infrequently led to the result that the signature vanishes. Graphological tests assist the chemical ones. But even the 'genuine' inscription—that is, the one which was added by the master himself immediately on the completion of the work—must not in all circumstances be regarded as valid and binding. A copyist may have taken it over from the archetype. When production was organized in a workshop—a circumstance always to be borne in mind—the master occasionally provided pictures, wholly or in part painted by his assistants, with his signature, as it were with a Trade Mark. 'Genuine' Bellini signatures occur on pictures which evidently are the work of other masters. Nobody troubled very much in the past about such a thing as spiritual ownership. Even the most venerable of all inscriptions, the celebrated stanza of four lines on the Ghent altarpiece, has very recently, for powerful reasons, been declared suspect.

— The inscription may be false, and its statement nevertheless accurate—so that in this case, a rare one no doubt, the objective criterion is not even decisive in a negative sense.

— Reliability is not to be expected from statements in inventories which, incidentally, contain authors' names only in exceptional cases, and from early writings. In the Prado at Madrid there is a *Madonna*, with the solemn information on the reverse of the panel to the effect that the city of Louvain in 1588 offered this work by Johannes Mabeus (Jan Gossaert, called Mabuse) as a present to King Philip II. I have not let this document prevent me from transferring the Madonna picture to Bernard van Orley. It is true that if it had been possible to fit this picture in among the works by Gossaert, then I would have welcomed the statement referred to as a valuable piece of evidence.

The inventories of princely galleries—such as those of Margaret of Austria, Vicereine of the Netherlands, or of King Charles I of England, and also, say, the notes made by Marcanton Michiel in North Italian houses—are to be utilized sceptically and to be taken seriously only to the extent that facts derived from style criticism do not contradict them.

Again, as to the measurably similar forms, the objectiveness of this criterion is questionable, and its importance as a clue is being exaggerated.

Enthusiasm is a state of mind natural to the lover of art—indeed, to him almost something normal. But it does produce a confusing effect. Morelli, who called himself Ivan Lermolieff, has written some notable sentences about Otto Mündler, whom he knew personally and valued highly. Mündler, says Morelli, relied upon his memory and his intuition; he made his decisions on the strength of the accidental impression produced by the whole. Enthusiasm sometimes lets down the critic badly. This may be read in the Introduction to Ivan Lermolieff's volume *Kunstkritische Studien in den Galerien zu München und Dresden* (1891). The Italian, masquerading as a Russian, emphasizes the shortcomings of his predecessors in order to recommend his analytical and 'scientific' method as a progress, an antidote. Again the ominous word 'accidental' is being used. I do not know why the impression of the whole of the picture should depend more on accident than the impressions of the individual portions, on the basis of which Morelli claimed and believed to judge.

It could probably be proved statistically that Morelli by applying his method—which he, not exactly logically, described as an 'experimental' one—made as many mistakes as Mündler depending on intuition. Nay, he would have made even more mistakes if he had applied his method consistently. The decisive factor is something that he too owes to intuition; and if we look closer, we shall find that he has utilized the much-praised method—the observation of measurably similar forms, notably the ears, the hands, the fingernails—less for the purpose of arriving at a verdict, than in order to provide evidence subsequently. He points to the individual forms in order to convince the reader of the justness of his attributions: but he, like every successful expert, has formed his opinion from the 'accidental' impression of the whole picture. He had a presentiment of this, and has even hinted at it, when on one occasion he assesses the value of his method—fairly accurately—as being an ancillary device, a means of checking.

The criterion of similarity of form is completely unavailing, once we are faced with the task of differentiating original from copy—thus to answer a question which, in the practice of connoisseurship, is a particularly frequent and burning one.

The verdict may be accurate, although the reasons, the attempt to present it as a compelling truth, established by analysis, appear misguided. It is noticeable that gifted experts in particular, who make their decisions with inner certainty, have little inclination to provide 'proof': they probably feel rather like Nietzsche, who said 'Am I then a barrel, carrying my foundations with me?'. False attributions are often presented with an excessive display of acuteness, and of arguments which sound irrefutable. False Raphael pictures are accompanied by whole brochures. The weaker the inner certainty, the stronger the need to convince others and oneself by lengthy demonstrations.

OBJECTIVE CRITERIA OF AUTHORSHIP

Enthusiastic lovers of art—at the same time mere amateurs—have contributed most and in the best fashion towards artistic reconstruction: they were, however, also exposed to the danger of making mistakes. Coldly analytical scholars make fewer mistakes; they perform, however, less in the way of positive perception; they discover less, with weaker flair. Morelli himself was, after all, an amateur in the best sense of the word; as a scholar he was rather affected.

— Morelli has ably provided psychological reasons for his method. Above all the painter renders the human figure in pose and movement, as well as the face, more particularly mouth and eyes, under the stress of emotional tension, in order to convey his vision to the spectator. In so doing he penetrates relatively deeply into the complexity of that which is individual; but he lapses into convention and routine when he draws parts of the human body, such as the ear or the hand, which seem to be of secondary importance as bearers of expression. The hand speaks more through its movement than through its shape. Moreover, precisely ear and hand are complicated formations, mastered by the draughtsman only with difficulty: so that the artist was tempted, by clinging to a formula, to evade the trouble of studying the given form in each case. Even great portrait painters of the 17th century, Van Dyck for example, have paid little attention to the individual shape of the hand.

— For other reasons the critic of style may be recommended to observe the drapery folds. The painter steps on to a domain of comparative freedom when, in conformity with his temperament and his condition of spirit, he lets the pliable textile undulate, ripple, break, swell, roll up, swing and flow out.

Costume, more particularly when elaborate and idealistic, made expression by means of sonorous melody possible for the artist. In studying the cast of drapery we almost become graphologists, and can deduce the personal temperament and even the momentary mood of the author from the flow of writing, from the arid, angular, measured, sober or exuberant, rushing, dramatically mobile and extravagant play of line. Evidence of the expressive force which can be breathed into the material of garments is provided by Grünewald and Hugo van der Goes.

The graphologist takes as his starting-point the fact that a writer must leave letters as much of their given form as legibility demands, but that he, free from this compulsion, is capable of spreading himself in the flourish, and in so doing expresses character, caprice and mood visibly. Also in the work of art, you can tell the difference between flourish and conventional sign. In the case of materials, costume, cut and sewn in such and such a fashion, resembles the letter; the play of folds, fluttering sashes, ends and ribbons resemble the flourish.

Mr. Berenson, who began as a grateful pupil of Morelli, has in a fragmentary article, published in

1902, under the title *Rudiments of Connoisseurship*, arranged the 'tests' under three headings, according as they are of use for the determination of authorship:—

First Group: Ear, Hand, Drapery fold, Landscape.
Second Group: Hair, Eye, Nose, Mouth.
Third Group: Cranium, Chin, Structure and Movement of the Human Figure, Architecture, Colour, Chiaroscuro.[1]

— This scheme is notable and is based on accurate thought: but it must not be applied as having universal validity. Tested in the practice of a connoisseur who has pre-eminently concerned himself with the Italian Quattrocento, it will, if used in connection with other periods, other manners of art, be partly unavailing. A Netherlandish painter of the 16th century may treat the landscape more variably, may invest it with more expression than architecture, so that, so far as he is concerned, architectural form becomes usable as a piece of evidence rather than landscape.

It must always be nicely calculated in each case whether there is predominance of habit and routine, or of observation of nature, individualizing characterization and expression of emotion. The more tense the will to achieve artistic form, the greater the variation.

[1] Bernhard Berenson, *The Study and Criticism of Italian Art*, second series, p. 144.

THE INTUITIVE VERDICT

The paradoxical idea that the master is recognizable where he has least drawn upon his force of expression, partly holds good. Argumentation providing reasons may successfully refer to the similarity of the ears; the act of intuitive arriving at a verdict springs from the impression of the whole. In the one case a master betrays himself; in the other he reveals himself.

XXV

ON INTUITION AND THE FIRST IMPRESSION

EVEN if attention deservedly goes to all the criteria which, with more or less justification, are
described as the 'objective', seemingly scientific ones,
and occupy a space disproportionately large in writings on art, decision ultimately rests with something
which cannot be discussed. To be sure, when we
come upon the concepts of intuition and self-evidence
—and every statement based upon style-criticism ultimately reaches and is wrecked by these concepts—
we resign as scholars and even as writers. A purely
emotional sense of conviction comes into play, and
pushes itself into the place of terse deduction. Perhaps every verdict, formulated on grounds of style
criticism, is nothing but a supposition; perhaps only
probability may be arrived at along this path.

Style-criticism inevitably reckons with probabili-
ties, builds up hypotheses. In order to make fruitful
use of such sensitive and delicate means, it is necessary to possess imagination and sincerity, a quality
which is often unavailing. The vain desire for a 'certain' result of one's studies is often stronger than the

love of truth. The scholar is able to provide reasons possessing a certain amount of probability for a 'determination'; proceeding, however, in the next chapter, he treats his supposition as an ascertained fact, and builds upon it further 'determinations'. We must insist that one should remain conscious of the degree of probability in each case, and proclaim it.

A hypothesis is something different from a supposition: it is an experiment. One may, tentatively, suppose even that which is improbable to be true, and draw deductions therefrom. A supposition gains in security if it can support tests of weight.

One should retain, and steel, one's courage of subjective opinion, but one should also sceptically and coolly put this opinion to the test. As in the case of a woman beloved, one should honour naïveté, but not let oneself be ruled by it.

The way in which an intuitive verdict is reached can, from the nature of things, only be described inadequately. A picture is shown to me. I glance at it, and declare it to be a work by Memling, without having proceeded to an examination of its full complexity of artistic form. This inner certainty can only be gained from the impression of the whole; never from an analysis of the visible forms.

This decision from feeling depends upon comparison, but not so much upon the recollection of such and such an authenticated signed or universally accepted work, as rather on an unconscious comparison of the picture to be ascribed with an ideal picture in my imagination. To gain, retain, refine and revive this ideal picture is the important thing, and hence it is advisable to devote as much time as ever possible to the contemplation, in full enjoyment, of the best and the authenticated works by a master; and on the other hand to devote little time to the problematic examples. Many experts act inversely, to their own detriment: they waste time and strength in examining dubious and insignificant pictures, and run the risk of confusing their taste and distorting their standards.

An ideal must not be fossilized: it must ever be kept capable of enrichment and change. It comprises not only such works as have been seen, but also such concealed possibilities as are contained in the gifts of a master. The idea of a master's capabilities becomes often all too early cut-and-dried: it should never be regarded as unchangeable.

If one has made a mistake—which is something that occasionally happens even to the gifted connoisseur—then one must radically and decisively evacuate the falsely judged work of art from one's memory and submit to a purge in the guise of the contemplation of indubitable works by the master. I remember the tragic case of an excellent and conscientious expert who once made a mistake. He was unable to summon sufficient courage and self-control to confess his mistake to himself; he searched for 'proofs' of his false attribution and as a result ended up in a false position with regard to the master, to whom he once by mistake had assigned something. As a result of this one mistake, which in itself was no disaster, he was bereft of pure and clear notion, and his judgment, at least so far as this master was concerned, lost certainty. And that *was* a disaster.

One should avoid as far as possible to link up an attribution based on style-criticism with another such attribution—in other words, to forge chains—since, of course, the risk of mistake is always there, and steps must be taken in advance to ensure that error does not produce error. A return to the secure starting-point remains imperative, to a centre from which attributions issue like rays.

Intuitive judgment may be regarded as a necessary evil. It is to be believed and disbelieved. Every sudden idea, however vague, may serve as basis for a fruitful hypothesis; only one must be ready to drop it as soon as it has proved itself incapable of sustaining weight.

In this mixture of bold initiative and equally determined resignation, of enthusiasm and scepticism, lies the fascination—exciting, keeping the spirit fresh and mobile—of work on the basis of style-criticism.

Intuition resembles the magnet needle, which shows us our way whilst it oscillates and vibrates.

In the case of some masters it is easy to find the place of security, where an idea of full complexity can be gained and the ideal given shape in our imagination. In the Hospital at Bruges we not only see works by

Memling, but experience his artistic activity, walk in his footsteps, measure the possibilities and limitations which were contained in his gifts. And it is with a similar profit that we leave the Frans Hals Museum at Haarlem, since there too the growth, the changes, the direction of an individual development, and the scope of a master are confided to us. Somewhat recklessly I venture to claim that *we learn to paint like Memling*, that is, to form the same visions as he. This imaginary pupilage, which naturally has nothing to do with realization—for, of course, we do not become capable of successful forging—obtains for us the inner certainty with which we decide: this must be by Memling, or that cannot be by him.

If someone tells me that he owns a *Still Life* by Frans Hals, signed and dated 1650, I conjure up—without ever having seen a *Still Life* by Frans Hals—an idea which serves me as a standard as to whether I accept or reject the picture when it is shown to me.

The work of art which I attribute, and my ideal picture of the master whose name I pronounce, stand to each other in the relationship of lock and key. The expert's weapon and possession are less photographs, books, or a dictionary of characteristics, than concepts of visual imagination, gained in pleasurable contemplation and retained by a vigorous visual memory. The capacity of memory is limited. Even a Wilhelm Bode, whose gifts as a connoisseur were of an unexampled manysidedness, was unavailing in many directions. The reliable and successful experts are specialists. One must summon courage to say 'I do not know' and reflect that he who attributes a picture wrongly reveals his ignorance of two masters—of the author, whom he does not recognize, and of the painter whose name he proclaims.

You cannot tell by the look of a verdict, based on style-criticism, whether it is correct or not. But with time its healthiness reveals itself by its capability of reproduction. A false verdict shows itself to be sterile. With the true something could be done, it was possible to build on it, and usually it was subsequently confirmed by knowledge gained along other paths, and from a different quarter.

The first impression is deeper than all subsequent ones, of different kind and of decisive importance. The first contact with a work of art leaves a profound imprint, if only because it is connected with excitement. The receptiveness of the eye is heightened by that which is new, strange, unexpected, different. And if the contact be repeated, it is the moment of recognition which produces the strongest effect. It seems therefore advisable to look at a picture periodically for six seconds rather than once for a whole minute. Inexperienced beginners, in order to study a picture thoroughly, stare at it so long that they no longer see anything: that is, no longer receive the impression of something arresting. The eye tires if it stays too long in the same place; that which is peculiar and specific assumes more and more the colour of that which is normal and incapable of being otherwise: the grace and advantage of the first impression are lost. Young art historians, who assiduously and intensively busy themselves with one master, without having seen much by others, lose the eye for the outline of their hero. Did not Montaigne in his wisdom think it worth while to note: 'When we want to judge the tonality of colour of a scarlet cloth, we must let our glance glide over it quickly and repeatedly.'

Every verdict on art is the result of a comparison, mostly made unconsciously. A heightening of the impression is obtained by means of contrasted effect. If I have seen a picture by Gerard Dou and then look at Rembrandt certain qualities of Rembrandt emerge; if, however, from Titian I turn to Rembrandt, I receive a different impression. To experiment in this fashion is advisable as an exercise. The greater the distance—as regards time, place or individual character—between the works of art which we confront with another, the more distinct is the impression of that which pertains to time and place; the closer they are to one another, the easier does it become to observe subtle differences, to draw, say, the dividing line between the master and his skilful imitator.

He who knows but one master knows him insufficiently. This inadequacy is often enough to be noted in works denoting a writer's debut, and particularly in theses for a doctorate.

XXVI

PROBLEMS OF CONNOISSEURSHIP

CHARLATANISM, the professional malady of experts, springs from the unstable nature of artistic judgment. The moment I formulate a statement in a way which goes beyond inner certainty, honesty begins to waver.

Dealers and collectors are not served by suppositions; they demand a positive decision. The expert not infrequently gets into a difficult position, since more is expected of him than he can honestly give. Let us say that he has recognized a picture as a work by Rembrandt. Out of confidence in him somebody acquires it at a high price. Later he arrives at the conviction that he has made a mistake. Even if his love of truth now overcomes his vanity, he is yet reluctant to harm someone who has believed in him. An expert of determined character did once, in such a situation, take over the doubtful picture at his own expense, but declared another time coldly and resolutely that the financial risk had to be borne by the person who had consulted him. Most people have less character; they do not confess their mistake or they try to confuse the hard facts, more particularly as they know from experience that their clients never forget a financial loss, whereas grateful memory is developed on a singularly slight scale.

— Every work of art has a financial value, which largely depends on the view taken of its authorship. This value also depends on its artistic value, which is difficult to assess, and in any case can be sent considerably up or down through the verdict of the expert. The expert comes up against financial interests and gets regrettably caught up in them.

I had an excellent friend who actually committed himself to the view that the science of art could be taken in hand seriously only after all works of art had become public property.

Since nobody can be called to account or produce proofs, since everything depends upon confidence and blind faith, it is authority which is demanded, claimed and striven for—at times even created artificially. The dealers have a natural interest in proclaiming the infallibility of the science, to which they appeal. A pearl merchant will always contend that it is child's play for him to tell genuine pearls from false.

The expert appears to the layman to be a magician and a worker of miracles. He thinks this part suits him and he becomes accustomed to indulge in the attitude of the conjurer. He is inclined to assert himself through rhetorical turns of speech; exclaiming, for instance, 'I put my hand in the fire that this is so', or else, 'Whoever does not see this, must be blind'. At times he tries to provide a basis for, and to strengthen his authority through, the appearance of heavy intellectual work and laborious research—since you may take credit for your industry, but not for your gifts, and many people like to take credit.

At the same time, let us be lenient towards human weaknesses. Satisfaction of his vanity, the exalting consciousness of authority and the power that goes with it, must compensate the expert for much that is disagreeable in his questionable profession. Honest recognition of positive performance hardly ever comes his way, least of all from his professional colleagues, who quote him only when they contradict him. Anything true that to-day he has been the first to find, is already to-morrow common property and at everybody's disposal. Mistakes survive, on the other hand, under his name and call up memories of him. Dubious things, which he was unable to attribute, are over and over again submitted to him with a silent reproach; while the works to which he, without being contradicted, has assigned such and such a name, disappear without further ado, and without earning for him any gratitude.

The quality of the works of art which drift about in the market is declining. The number of the dealers and agents who want to live by the sales in the art market grows continuously. The difference in value between a picture by Rembrandt and one by Ferdinand

Bol is increasing. The hunt for valuable things becomes ever madder and more relentless. Connoisseurship becomes more and more specialized, takes on the character of a mystery, so that even a highly regarded and experienced dealer can no longer say to his customers: 'I regard the picture as a work by Titian and assume the guarantee; there is no need for an expert opinion'. All these are circumstances which contribute to an increase in the power of the expert, and to the danger of misusing this power.

'Expertizing' is felt to be mischievous, but as things are it is bound to be ineradicable and a necessary evil. The need to establish whether a picture really is the work of Rembrandt by consulting an authority, a disinterested and conscientious writer of expert opinions, appears urgent. The difficulty lies in the regrettable uncertainty as to who is a well-informed and honest writer of expert opinions. All suggestions made, and measures taken, in order to combat the degeneration of 'expertizing' have done more harm than good. Museum officials have thus in many places been forbidden to give written opinions, which means that a number of the best experts have been excluded, and the field has been thrown open to unofficial, professional writers of expert opinions. As a result the average standard of truth of the expert opinions has declined. The official may pronounce himself only verbally. The verbal opinion is naturally formulated with less sense of responsibility than the written opinion; and, moreover, it is usually distorted when subsequently handed on. The French institution of the *experts* as government officials has certainly proved its worth in the administration of justice, since a financial guarantee is linked with an attribution put forward; but it has not succeeded in asserting itself against free, un-attached, specialized connoisseurship; it has been unable to replace it or eliminate the latter.

There is no choice but optimistically to rely upon the fact that ignorance and unscrupulousness will gradually be discovered in the circles of the collectors, and that the dealers as a result will be induced to exercise circumspection in the choice of the writers of expert opinions.

The complaints regarding frivolous and untruthful expert opinions are all too justified. They have caused a reaction, so that timorous minds nowadays go to extremes in judging negatively or with reserve. The people concerned say 'no' in order not, at all events, to be confused with the 'yes-men'. Now prudence is not only the mother of wisdom but also the daughter of ignorance. What must be done is to steer the right course between the rocks of a conciliatory complaisance on the one hand and a negative attitude, on principle, on the other.

XXVII

THE ANALYTICAL EXAMINATION OF
PICTURES

I HAVE compared intuitive judgment to swimming in a deep river, and have admitted that occasionally we, even in shallow waters, tread on firm ground, namely, as soon as we dissect the work of art. You cannot explain a witticism without murdering it. And the position is the same with regard to the work of art. Nevertheless, the fear of elusive, mysterious and incalculable intuition is over and over again conducive to reconsideration, testing and checking by means of dividing and dissecting visual action. By establishing the causes of the total impression through analysis we, in any case, enrich our knowledge. And one should not underestimate knowledge. He who knows most, sees most. One should not, however, on the other hand over-estimate knowledge. It is of no use to him who cannot see.

We address questions to the work of art. In order to be as complete as possible, it may be useful to have a questionnaire ready.

THE PROBLEM OF ORIGINAL SIZE

First of all a query which is often forgotten: Is the work of art preserved for us within its original boundaries, that is complete? Is it a whole, or only a fragment, say the wing of an altarpiece? Our judgment as regards the composition depends upon the answer. If it is a question of an easel picture, painted on wood or canvas, we examine the panel to see if it is present in its original extent, and investigate similarly the canvas. The panel was usually, notably in the Low Countries during the 17th century, reduced in thickness by working neatly wedge-fashion towards the four edges. The uniform, prismatic cut is notable as a characteristic. The painters of the 15th century laid the gesso ground on the wooden panel which was already enclosed by its frame. The doughy matter as a result formed a ridge along the edges of the frame. If this ridge is visible at all four sides, then we may be sure of possessing the picture to its original extent. The canvas shows frequently old colour on the edges bent across the chassis. This is an indication that the canvas has subsequently been stretched on a new chassis, and that the picture surface has been reduced in consequence.

Like naturalists we study the materials—the species of wood, the texture of the canvas and the pigments. We gain as a result details of evidence helpful towards localizing and dating. In the Low Countries and in Northern Germany one used almost exclusively oak panels, mostly of slight thickness; in Southern

Germany mostly lime wood or—especially in the Alpine districts—the streaky wood of the conifers; in France, apart from oak, the wood of nut-trees; in Italy poplar wood in relatively thick boards. If a picture by Dürer is painted on oak, we may surmise that it was executed in the Netherlands, that is in 1520 or 1521.

Pictures painted on wood have been transferred to canvas by means of a procedure which, used in 18th-century France but sparingly, has of late become fairly frequent, notably in Russia. If the climate is dry —for example in the latter country as well as in America—generally as a result of excessive heating the panel warps and causes blistering of the layer of colour. In order to prevent the colour from flaking off one resorts to the radical, at times very risky, procedure of planing the wood on the reverse completely away, and substituting for it an elastic canvas. If the gesso ground—which of course is handled with delicacy—is of a certain thickness, then a relatively favourable result may be achieved. The picture, mounted on canvas, in that case retains its texture and lustre; in other words, qualities which are characteristic of the panel pictures. Frequently, however, transferring entails a partial destruction, a perforation of the original body of colour, and disfiguring restoration becomes necessary. Of the pictures that we possess from the brush of Jan van Eyck, no fewer than four have undergone the operation, surviving it more or less satisfactorily; namely, the two wings of an altarpiece in the Metropolitan Museum of Art in New York, the *Annunciation* in the National Gallery in Washington, the *Crucifixion* in Berlin and the *Madonna with Saints* belonging to Baron Robert de Rothschild of Paris.

One may read everywhere that Jan van Eyck invented oil painting. Posthumous praise, more or less erroneous as to content, is never groundless: it points to an extraordinary performance, or at any rate to an epoch-making event, which then was personified. Now the pictures of Jan van Eyck undoubtedly look different from the ones that were produced before, or by others at the same time. And—a notable point —the Netherlandish followers of Jan van Eyck, who took the method over from him, were unable to utilize it in the same degree as he: could not as perfectly bring it into harmony with their method of vision. We must therefore assume a personal venture during the universal crisis in the conception of the world about 1420. I should like, however, to avoid the expression 'invention'. In any case it would be a mistake to assume that Jan van Eyck achieved the novel effect because, and after, he had invented something. On the contrary he developed the new technique because the traditional methods did not correspond to his vision. The find was result, not cause. The decisive and primary thing was the wish to achieve *clair-obscur*, richness of detail, gradation of light, a *matière* which glowed jewel-like and was translucid—in other words, what the painter had been the first to perceive and find beautiful. That which is called oil painting is something that genius detected in nature: and it found the means to realize its vision.

What is known as oil colour was not used for painting on canvas in the Low Countries before 1530. The painted 'cloths' which were produced there before that date are painted in water-colour, and cannot be confused with pictures transferred from panel to canvas.

It is easy to tell the difference between the relatively opaque, cool tempera, which obtained almost through the whole 15th century in Italy, and the deeply lustrous, liquid, repeatedly stratified 'oil colour', which, ever since the days of Jan van Eyck, was favoured in the North of Europe.

A chemical investigation of pigments permits deductions regarding the age of a picture; since the emergence into use and the discovery of certain pigments are historically demonstrable. As far as I am aware, this research has been carried farthest by Dr. A. P. Laurie in his volume *The Pigments and Mediums of the Old Masters* (1914).

The scientific methods lately applied with eagerness—X-ray photography, irradiation by means of the quartz lamp, enormous enlargement, photography with powerful side-lighting—supplement the report given by the naked eye, and often perform use-

ful services. More particularly do they supply a diag-
nosis of the medical case, without which a prudent
restorer should not proceed to the operation. The
Manuel de la conservation des peintures, published in
1938 by the *Office International des Musées*, conveys very
graphically information concerning all the devices of
physical and chemical investigation. In so far as it is a
question of the actual materials, the refinements of
observation denote a progress which should be grate-
fully welcomed. But when it is a question of artistic
effect, there exists the danger that the scholars, who
busy themselves so intensely with that which is invisible to the naked eye, lose the capacity to receive
an impression of that which is visible. Insensitive
observers acquire the right to take part in a discussion
about artistic matters: they take the watch to pieces
in order to study the works. And the watch no longer
goes.

It is possible to judge from the manner of painting,
the individual handling of the brush, in cases where the
method of work is patent in deep and distinct traces:
as for instance in the late works by Rembrandt or in
the coloured sketches by Rubens. Temperament, *élan*,
or tiredness betray themselves in the manner—vehe-
ment, decisive or else cautiously feeling its way—
in which paint has been applied. The nearer we get
to modern times, the more openly does the painter
reveal himself in the flow of handwriting. Dr. Laurie,
in his book just referred to, demonstrates very in-

structively, on the basis of some examples dating from the 17th, 18th and 19th centuries, the handling of the brush by means of considerable enlargements. But even where the colour surface, apparently self-contained after the fashion of enamel, seems to tell nothing about the method of execution, as for instance in the panel pictures of the 15th century, patient observation is capable of establishing a good deal concerning the method of execution. The surface is mostly not so uniformly smooth as it seems at first sight. Some pigments are spread, often as if they had run out, with heavier body than others over the picture surface. Each workshop had its own special procedures. Individual methods of applying the colours can be made out, even if, within the craftsmanlike formula of working which obtained during the 15th century, they reveal themselves comparatively indistinctly.

The X-ray photography—at present employed with passion, often usefully, not infrequently to no good purpose—reveals that which, invisible to the naked eye, lies under the top layer of colour; makes it possible to recognize *pentimenti*—that is, artists' corrections on second thoughts; and is capable of teaching the experienced connoisseur a lot. But it confuses the inexperienced one and lures him to false deductions. —— The condition of the picture is of the greatest importance. We must possess a clear notion as to how much of the original work is present; how much maybe is wanting, or replaced or covered up by retouching; what is rubbed off; what is altered by decomposition, by darkening or by opaque layers of varnish. *A priori* it is to be expected that no old picture should stand before our eyes in flawless condition, exactly as it issued from the workshop of the master. These questions, if ever asked, are but imperfectly answered by most people, even by otherwise excellent connoisseurs; and hence their judgment often has an insecure basis. The study, unfortunately becoming ever more popular, of photographs at the writing-desk can least of all confer or strengthen the capacity to judge the condition of a picture correctly. The best training is provided by frequent visits to the studios of the restorers.

A characteristic of good condition is the uniform effect of the whole of the picture. The experienced eye runs over the surface, enjoys the unbroken harmony or becomes irritated and suspicious by contradictions. Opaque passages alongside of transparent ones; clear and distinct ones alongside of murky ones; delicate drawing alongside of careless; in a word, discord of every kind allows us to deduce the partial destruction of the original, defects and repainting. Uniform rubbing of the entire picture surface is seldom met with, since, of course, the pigments have opposed more or less vigorous resistance to the destructive forces.

In order to establish the degree of darkening, confusing and discolouring through layers of varnish which have gone opaque or are in a definitely unhealthy condition, it is advisable to examine the lightest portions—say, in the white draperies—for the purpose of measuring how closely the highest light in the picture approaches pure white. In this fashion one obtains an approximate idea of the degree of disfiguration.

The method, invented by the late Herr Pettenkofer, of using spirit vapours in order to make the unhealthy 'dead' varnish once more transparent, to 'regenerate' it, is in many cases a useful procedure, at least for the purpose of gaining a clear idea of the condition of the original layer of colour. Lately this method, previously eagerly employed, is neglected in favour of X-ray photography and irradiation by means of the quartz lamp. The most recently invented method is naturally for choice regarded as a magic formula.

The layer of varnish—even if it gives the picture a warmth of tone which was not intended by the old masters—cannot under all conditions be regarded as denoting a decrease of value. It gives the picture on the one hand a self-contained effect and restfulness, and on the other a picturesque 'mellowness'—in other words qualities which at any rate to our eyes, the eyes of our time, are occasionally advantageous to the effect of the picture. There exists such a thing as unintentional increase of the picturesque effect. Not

20. HUGO VAN DER GOES, ADORATION OF THE SHEPHERDS ('THE PORTINARI ALTARPIECE')

Florence, Uffizi

everything that the centuries have done to the layer of colour cometh of evil—not even the *craquelure*, which is almost inevitable. It softens and reduces, in a welcome fashion, hardness, smoothness and emptiness, entirely apart from the fact that wrinkles and symptoms of age once and for all are indissolubly linked up with our idea of the venerable art of the past. There is such a thing as *patina*, as *aerugo nobilis*, also on pictures. It is said that colours and tones, as years go by, amalgamate.

As an object of study the *craquelure* is instructive, since it can tell us something about the date of the picture. Notably anyone who wants to be able to expose forgeries will do well to take a serious interest in this remarkable feature. The eye must train itself to tell the difference between that tattered condition of the gesso preparation and the layer of colour, which has come into being organically, and that which has been produced wilfully; the necessarily natural-born change from that which has been produced artificially. Nature, in alliance with time, has more phantasy than the human spirit. Hence the natural *craquelure* throbs with rich variety, whilst monotony and pedantic repetition mark the arbitrary, intentionally irregular one.

Arc-like circular cracks, which recall the spider's web, are notably characteristic of the canvas pictures of the 18th century.

The unscholarly pictorial technique of the 19th

century has often brought it about that the tattered layer of colour shows broad channels. This peculiarity has often made it possible to recognize forgeries or modern copies. But that this characteristic is not infallible became patent when the *Madonna with the Sweet Pea* at Cologne, on the strength of the cracks, was declared—most erroneously—to be a forgery dating from the 19th century.

There are even cases in which the *craquelure* tells us something about the personal manner of painting of such and such a master, and is to be taken into account as a criterium of authorship. Palma Vecchio's device is the enamel of the body of colour, whereby he achieves an extraordinary lustre of the flesh and distinguishes himself among his Venetian contemporaries. The shadows of the flesh show with him a gritty decomposition, which produces the effect of picturesque softness and mellowness.

Anton Graff's pictures show, as a result of special experiments in pictorial technique, a shrivelling of the colour surface which recalls rough leather.

In the pictures by Pieter Pourbus I have hardly ever been able to discover *craquelure*.

The criteria, obtained through science, help in any case to fix the time and place of the work of art and, as a result, indirectly further the determination of authorship, since through the classification concerned the circle of the masters to be considered is narrowed down and the discovery of the author is facilitated.

194

A TENTATIVE QUESTIONNAIRE

A questionnaire, aiming at completeness with regard to pictorial expression and language of form, is something I do not desire to draft. It must be adapted to the character of the work of art from case to case. One cannot address the same questions to a Botticelli as to a Manet. A scheme with indications may here suffice.

Iconography.

How has the subject been treated previously elsewhere? The relationship with tradition. From the legend of such and such a saint it is often possible to draw conclusions regarding the locality and date of the picture. Some saints were venerated only or predominantly in certain cities.

Composition.

Symmetry, more or less reduced in rigidity. The disposition of the figures in the plane or the depth of space. The relationship of the figure to space as indicated by landscape or figures.

Architecture, Ornament.

From the style of the buildings one may not in all circumstances deduce the date of the picture: it is only the *terminus post quem* which is at all times fixed. In the 15th and 16th centuries architectural forms of the past—notably those of the Romanesque period—were often imitated in order to provide historical colour to the rendering of a sacred or legendary subject.

4. *Language of Form.*

    Proportions of the figures, motifs of movemen
    expression of sentiment, colour.

5. *Costume, Arms and Armour.*

    Knowledge of the history of costume can help cor
    siderably in dating a picture. It is to be noted th
    the Old Masters by no means always cling to th
    costume of their own period; but on the contrar
    in order to suggest distance of time, and whil
    knowing little about older costume, have more c
    less indulged in phantasies.

In an exemplary fashion and with the simplici
peculiar to him Ludwig Scheibler has characterize
the Cologne masters of the 15th century analyticall
in his memorable doctoral dissertation of 1880. I
however, someone imagined that he would only hav
to learn the letterpress of the book by heart in orde
to be able to determine the authorship of Cologr
pictures he would be guilty of a sorry mistake. It
one's own impression of the entire picture whic
decides; the dissecting contemplation serves at mo:
as check and argumentation.

XXVIII

ON THE USE OF PHOTOGRAPHY

PHOTOGRAPHY and the publishing of pictures are continuously on the up grade; conveniently accessible archives contain enormous quantities of reproductions, while the possibilities of travel are restricted for many students. As a result style-criticism is being practised in an ever increasing degree on the basis of photographs. The evil consequences of this condition of things are concealed from no one. The very fact of possessing a photographic reproduction—or the certainty of being able to obtain one—reduces the interest which is devoted to the original. One should picture to oneself how the lover of art must have felt when he found himself face to face at Castelfranco with Giorgione's altarpiece, at a time when no photographs of it existed, and when he looked upon this first contact with the picture, as maybe, also the last one. How his emotion must have increased receptiveness!

It is true that the photograph has become indispensable, and an invaluable auxiliary; but its use must be governed by discretion and moderation. It must not

push itself into the place of the original. We mus
have a clear perception of that which it can perform.

The risk of confusing original and copy has beer
immensely increased in the case of the facsimile re
productions of drawings, which seemingly are indis
tinguishable from the originals. The technical me
thods which are necessary in order to achieve such
similarity, entail drastic intervention by means o
retouching. The simple photograph, as supplied b
the camera, is to be preferred to the facsimile repro
duction as a dependable, even if incomplete, report
Colour plates of pictures are to be used with pro
found suspicion.

The ordinary photographic print, the half-ton
block made from it—not to speak of the lately all
too-fashionable cylindrical photogravures with thei
sham chiaroscuro—at least do not belie their own in
sufficiency. The colour is lacking, and a great dea
is lost as a result. The gradation of tone can, thank
to technical improvements, be reproduced with som
measure of success. As to size and proportion, fals
ideas are conveyed to us. And these shortcomings ar
not even always made good to some extent by an in
dication of the real size.

Apart from colour the reproduction lacks also th
texture of the pigments, their lustre, their brilliance
their smoothness or roughness, their grain, their im
pasto. The indivisible effect, which springs from th
whole, cannot be conveyed when the reproduction i

so fragmentary. The important preliminary question of the condition of the picture can be answered from a reproduction only in cases of drastic disfigurement. All these disadvantages apply also to lantern slides, which are so freely used in university teaching.

Photographs should be used in order to awaken and strengthen recollection of the originals: as a basis of judgment they are to be excluded as far as possible. They will render good service in presenting an argument, and in order to provide supplementary reasons for an opinion formed in front of the picture itself.

XXIX

ON PERSONALITY AND ITS DEVELOPMENT

OUR courage to proceed to the determination of authorship—whether we go by intuition or by analysis and 'objective' criteria—we derive from a belief that creative individuality has an unchangeable core. We start on the assumption that the artist—whatever he experiences, whatever impulses he receives, however he may change his abode—at bottom remains the same, and that something which cannot be lost reveals itself in his every expression. This belief is often shaken by practical experience, but remains indispensable as a compass on the journey of the critic of style. If we stand in front of two works by the same master which, although both authenticated and for certain reasons indubitable, yet differ greatly from one another, then the question as to what can, after all, be determined as the common denominator does take us into the very depth of things, and into the very core of personality.

In spite of many disappointments we persevere in our endeavour to discover something that is unchangeably solid, and in so doing often get into the position of a man who peels an onion and in the end realizes that an onion consists of peelings.

CHARACTER IN LITERATURE

On reading novels and autobiographies one cannot help noticing the fact that the less important figures —now on, now off the stage—are drawn definitely and distinctly, whereas the hero—who in novels not unfrequently is identical with the author—strikes us as indefinite, changeable, incalculable, not to say devoid of character. The more there is drawing within the contour, the less effective and expressive does the silhouette become. A description of character—which always tends somewhat to caricature—achieves success relatively easily, if it does not go below the surface. One can go so far as to claim that all human instincts and impulses are concealed in every human being, and are at war with one another; that, according to circumstances, this or that impulse moves towards the outside and becomes noticeable, in action and behaviour, as a characteristic. The better you get to know a human being, the more surprises do you experience from him. But however sceptically you may be prejudiced, you must, however, presuppose a disposition of character in the individual relation of the impulses to one another, in the predominance of such and such instincts and inclinations; and a direction of development caused thereby.

I try to set up a scale in which the qualities, revealed actively and passively by a human being, appear arranged according to their stability, as springing more or less compulsorily from his disposition. I choose for the diagram in question, the shape of the star. In the centre is the solid core, a point. From this centre there issue rays, which undulate and oscillate all the more vigorously the greater their distance from the focus. If I then draw concentric circles round the centre, I obtain zones, of which the innermost one, with relatively straight rays close to the focus, contains the least mobile qualities; the outermost one, on the other hand, contains the qualities which are most powerfully shaken by experiences, by contacts, by demands. The ray passes thus from necessity to caprice.

The difficulty begins as soon as we have to deal practically with the cut-and-dried scheme. We expect that, say, courage to live, phlegm, melancholia, ethical forces, strength of will, timorousness as well as intellectual faculties, belong in the innermost zone; whereas everything that has been learnt or taken over is to be relegated to the outermost zone. The average human being, however, acts and behaves predominantly in accordance with habit, norm, general custom; and it is only in exceptional situations and for unusual reasons, that he reveals, surprising us, his personal character.

It is a question by itself whether and to what a degree the artist gives visible expression in his work to his deep-rooted qualities, from the innermost zone. Habit may reveal itself more distinctly than individual impulse in specific and significant features. We often decide the question of authorship on the strength of characteristics whose connection with the core of personality is scarcely provable. The great master, the genius, brings more out of the depth into the light than the master of low or medium rank. Of course, no one is going to contradict certain prophecies, based upon the knowledge of independent, creative personalities. Michelangelo can have produced nothing petty, Raphael nothing coarse, Holbein nothing vague, Dürer nothing frivolous. But already if someone were to lay it down that a master so delicate, so concerned about dignity and decorum as Van Dyck, could never have aimed at brutality of effect, it would be possible to contest this by reference to certain works by the master. In this case we might console ourselves with the reflection that Van Dyck, with his adaptability, his assiduity, his consciousness, does not belong to the circle of the great. But who belongs to it? And who belongs to it during the whole of his development? Once Rembrandt's emotional purity, spiritual freedom and inability to compromise have revealed themselves to us from the works of his late period, we stand startled and puzzled before certain cheaply striking and mannered productions of his early period. His genius, his personality rose but slowly, freed itself from and left behind but gradually, such formulae, tendencies and aspirations as were limited in time and space.

The strong man grows from his own strength, becomes increasingly the one that he is; the weak man resembles a plastic material which is being shaped. Hence it is a problem, in one case to get to understand a personality sympathetically, in the other to note the surrounding circumstances, the style of the period, the demands that were being made. In the first place it is principally intuition which decides as regards the 'must'; in the second it is analysis and manysided knowledge which exercise similar action with regard to intention. The experts of the second rank can deal successfully mainly with artists of the second rank. The expert's relation to genius is that of the faithful disciple, to talent that of a cunning detective.

We are entitled to expect that in all the productions of a master the degree of spiritual giftedness—apprehended in a work of art as level of merit—remains a constant. In conformity therewith the connoisseur makes his decision in a positive or negative sense, and traces in awkward beginnings the possibilities contained in a given disposition. For each master he draws in his imagination a boundary line which may be reached and not crossed. That which is positive is less deceptive than that which is negative. A man of brains is far more likely to say something silly once, than a fool is likely ever to say anything intelligent.

If we conceive individual nature not as something that exists but something that grows—and that, of course, is what we have begun to do—then we get over many difficulties. The great masters begin undemonstratively, as it were in a chrysalis: they start on a line marked by their predecessors. We may recall the discussions as to the boundary line between Giorgione and Titian, or as regards Albrecht Dürer's Bâle period. The controversy about such problems continues for decades without being settled. If all pictures by Rembrandt had been lost, except one of 1627 and one of 1660, it would be impossible to connect them with one another solely on the basis of style criticism. Only when we are familiar with the chain of many links, which makes up the *œuvre*—and that is the case with Rembrandt—can we join beginning to end.

The personality forms itself gradually, and we must see to it that it forms itself before our eyes. All connoisseurship aims at biography. The Ariadne thread of biographical dates makes it possible for us to find our way. The chronological order helps us considerably. That which a master once has achieved cannot be completely lost by him. Every creation can be regarded as the result of all preceding ones.

Greco can only be understood if we know that he went from the Near East to Venice, and from there to Toledo.

Sooner or later, the master finds the path which is in conformity with his nature, and thereupon follows it more or less in a straight line. Capacity for evolution is a characteristic of powerful gifts. Those who are great find themselves at the end far away from their starting-point.

ON PERSONALITY AND ITS DEVELOPMENT

Historians have learnt to reckon with the possibility of change, but not with its necessity. A master cannot, strictly speaking, produce the same in 1520 as in 1510, unless he imitates himself, in which case paralysis, dullness and ossification are bound to become noticeable. When growing ceases, decay begins.

The position is seldom so favourable as in the case of Memling and of Frans Hals. It is generally not made so easy for us to form an idea of the development of a master in one locality. We are faced with necessity of building up through our imagination, as far as possible, for each master something like the Hospital of St. John or the Frans Hals Museum. At one time there was only one work—the Portinari altarpiece—available to tell us something about Hugo van der Goes. One point in his career was thus fixed. I then compare the Portinari altarpiece, whose date is known, with earlier and with contemporary works by other masters—especially such as were settled in the same neighbourhood—and already in so doing gain an idea of the direction which the personality of the Ghent master was bound to follow. I am able to carry a line through the point denoted by the Portinari altarpiece in two directions, and thus to further the aggregation of other works. It is an advantage if, as in this case, the fixed point has its place approximately in the middle of the artist's career.

It is to be presupposed that Hugo van der Goes, as an independent master, highly capable of developient, enlarged and widened his form more and more; nd this makes us inclined to consider pictures of mall size—like those in the Vienna Gallery—as comaratively early works. But, as I remarked when peaking of size and proportion, the painters were ot free in the choice of dimensions. The Vienna anels do not show a natural, congenital smallness; hey suggest a reduction of size, due to compulsion. They grow in one's recollection. Their content of rm and knowledge of form are in conformity with irger proportions. Hence we begin to doubt whether ve really are concerned with youthful productions. I el more certain in regarding the *St. Anne, the Virgin nd Child*, the modest work in the Brussels Gallery, as relatively early production, because in this instance he volume of sound seems to be in conformity with he size of the instrument. If I place the Portinari ltarpiece and the Monforte altarpiece—thus two riptychs of approximately similar dimensions—next o one another, I believe I am entitled to deduce that he Monforte altarpiece is the later work, because in t the language of form seems even more of a match or the monumental proportions. This is, by the way, ot the general opinion.

A statement 'this work, from its character of style, s the work of a youthful master' is audacious, and nreliable. One may say, with more justification and efiniteness: 'This picture by the master was painted arlier than that one; it is, comparatively speaking, a

youthful work.' Only with difficulty should one de
cide to say: 'The master cannot have painted this pic
ture'; it is already easier to opine 'he cannot have
painted it in 1470'. The more we know about the
master's destiny, the more extensive the material of
examples we have brought together, the more does
the circle of possibilities and mistakes contract, the
greater become the calm and determination with
which we classify and build up.

General rules as to individual growth, valid always
and everywhere, may only be formulated with extreme
caution and reserve; they assist the critic of style
solely in conjunction with far-reaching knowledge of
biographical dates. Titian, Rembrandt and Frans Hals
have followed paths which run approximately parallel.

Youth, quickly changing, is bold and shy, arrogant
and dejected; the age of man's maturity witnesses
solid work for the benefit of the outside world and
the reaching of an understanding with conditions that
exist; old age—if untroubled by illness, want or care
—has reached clarity and is equably cheerful. Youth
learns to look, old age to overlook. At first hesitation
while walking briskly; then an unperturbed advance;
finally, rest. Healthy natures show, more or less clearly,
this sequence.

One may form for oneself an ideal of organic awak
ening, maturing and decaying; one may postulate for
each age certain instincts and impulses as predomin
ating; one must, however, also bear in mind the

208

many forces which cut across a normal development, such as illnesses, opposition from the world outside, uprooting, the growth of bitterness owing to lack of success. Prejudice—frequently enough confirmed, for that matter—causes us to presuppose that form, as an individual artist develops, becomes ampler and poorer in detail. It is, however, perfectly possible for the taste of the period—which terrorizes notably the feebler talents—to direct precisely an opposite course to be followed; as was for instance the case in Holland during the second half of the 17th century. The strong men pursue their path in opposition to the general movement, as for example Frans Hals and Rembrandt, who at the end, isolated and uncomprehended, rose above their contemporaries. Other great masters, like Raphael or Titian, seem to cover long distances in step with their own generation, though in such cases it is difficult to define how powerfully they themselves determine the taste of the period. Many masters have died prematurely, having had no time to age organically.

That the mature master works with wise superiority, relying more upon experience and memory than upon observation, and taking a general view of things; that the ageing master may reach the point at which he becomes his own imitator: this is a law of artistic nature with which we have to reckon.

All human activity is governed by the law of inertia. It is only possible for strong forces—such as fanaticism, coercive richness of imagination pertaining to genius, ambition, dissatisfaction with one's own perform- ance—to paralyse the deep-rooted compulsion to repeat a movement, to follow the same path once again; and such strong forces generally wane with the passing of years. Every action demands, when per- formed for the second time, a lesser expenditure of force than the first time. Habit runs through all ar- tistic activity, and more particularly when a master of mature years can look back upon success, upon re- cognition. Repetition, as the inner tension decreases, is eventually conducive to mannerism.

We speak of mannerism as opposed to style when we come upon forms that are conventional, imitated from the artistic production of others or oneself, not derived from vision: that is, upon forms that strike us as artificially made, instead of natural-born. An in- structive example of the groundlessness of manner- istic motifs is offered by the fluttering terminations of draperies, favoured in Antwerp about 1520; they wave and whirl without reference to an air current or any other motive power.

The assumption of a normal development proves fruitful even in cases where, as frequently experienced, observation testifies against it. Questions such as why Lucas Cranach was not impelled towards the grand style, the picturesque; why Albrecht Altdorfer in his maturity became a miniaturist; which forces coun- teracted the natural unfolding—such questions are conducive to the study of surroundings and the conditions of the times, and facilitate the construction of biographies. The general tragic German fate counteracted the organic individual development, particularly fatally in the case of Cranach, but more or less in the entire production of his time. Only the genius of Grünewald seems not to have been hemmed in by the repressive forces.

Generally speaking the art historian cannot exercise sufficient caution in dealing with the concept of law; he should content himself with deducing points of view from his observations—and from these points of view he then gains further observations. The naturalist may argue: 'if this is what happened in that case, the same thing must happen in this case'. We, however, must limit ourselves to saying: 'if this is what happened in that case, the same thing *may* happen in this case, and we will now see if that is so'.

At times the following phases outline themselves: first, clinging to inherited form, tradition and theory; then, awakening of the individuality coupled with independent observation of nature; finally, autonomous handling of the possessions of form thus acquired. The path runs from the manner of others, *via* observation of nature, to one's own manner. The frequently defective knowledge with regard to youthful works may seemingly restrict the number of cases in which this scheme is applicable. We know, for instance, nothing about the beginnings of Lucas Cranach, who perhaps reveals himself to us only in the second phase of his development.

The works belonging to the old age of the greatest masters all share a sublime and transfigured timelessness.

Only if the destiny of a master with all its changes is known to us in every detail—and our knowledge never extends thus far—would we be in a position to apply general rules to the individual case without violating the latter.

The ultimate wish, hardly ever fulfilled in the case of the art historian, is directed towards the discovery of the law in conformity with which personality began to be formed. We should like to deduce from the seed, by which we understand the early work, all possibilities of development. The more original the work of a master, the closer do we expect to approach this goal, which is never reached but must never be left out of sight.

XXX

ON THE ANONYMOUS MASTERS, THE MEDIUM MASTERS AND THE LESSER MASTERS

THE great masters, with whom historians for choice concern themselves in the hope of coming across those forces which were the decisive ones in history, are—exceptions apart—at the same time those who produced some effect already upon their contemporaries—be it the effect of admiration or amazement—so that repute beyond the grave has penetrated into early writings. It is true that traditional fame must not, without further ado, provide the historian with his standards—not to speak of the lover of art. Accents have been distributed from prejudice, according to the standpoint of the chronicler. Vasari's partiality for Florence is even now productive of confusion.

Some masters have by signing their works provided for their fame beyond the grave. Martin Schongauer may not be greater than the Master of the Hausbuch; he has, however, as a historical personality got in before the anonymous artist, precisely because with his initials he made things easy for the historians and forced himself upon them. It is the great artists concerning whom we learn, at any rate, something with regard to time and place, life and influence; so that we construct the edifice of style-criticism with the aid of a biographical scaffolding.

There are, however, cases in which we build without a scaffolding, as it were stitch and crochet, instead of carrying out an embroidery on a given ground. The study of masters who owe their existence and provisional names to style-criticism, can be described as the march past of connoisseurship. In this endeavour we must take as our starting-points the well-known masters, whose historical position is firmly established and who, like milestones, make it possible to assign places to the anonymous in their vicinity and between them. Let me quote as an instance a panel picture, on oak, displaying a composition which in part goes back to Roger van der Weyden, and a language of form which recalls Memling. The subject is St. Donatian, the patron of Bruges. Hence it is possible to deduce: Bruges, second half of the 15th century. I look, not without success, for pictures by the same hand in Bruges churches and find one bearing the date 1480. The dated picture looks earlier than the one first considered. I now have at my disposal not only the characteristics of a personal style but also an idea of the direction taken by the painter's evolution, and can, with growing certainty, increase the *œuvre* of the anonymous master and put it into order. Under all circumstances we work with a yearning for biography.

The 'Master of the Death of the Virgin', before his real name was known, stood before the eyes of art lovers as a personality definitely outlined. Time and place, the direction taken by his development, and a considerable *œuvre* had been deduced without the help of documentary or literary tradition. As his *œuvre* grew, the more data and supports emerged, enabling us to evolve the hypothesis that he was identical with Joos van Cleve, a painter about whom something was to be found in early writings. That which had been conquered by means of style-criticism tallied happily with the biographical data. Finally, the Cleve arms in an altarpiece, together with the initials J. v. B. (Joos van Beke), transformed the surmise into ascertained fact.

We experience difficulty in keeping up with the great, and worry lest we be hoaxed by the lesser men. The talent of medium or lesser strength disguises itself, masquerades, intentionally does now this, now that. Genius changes from inner necessity, talent for a reason. Evolution in one case follows its course in accordance with laws, which it is one of the tasks of a biographer to discover; in the other by fits and starts, with sudden changes, whose causes the biographer endeavours to establish.

The modest artists find mostly, after a period of

feeling their way, a manner to which they cling complacently, especially if some success is vouchsafed them. They make least trouble for style-criticism. The assiduous and ambitious men of medium stature, especially in a critical period of universal change of style, are capable of driving the expert to despair. The task of bringing their *œuvre* together is often insoluble, unless inscriptions or 'objective' data of another kind lend their assistance. An example of histrionic capacity for change is afforded by Bernard van Orley. As regards the medium and lesser masters, one should always bear in mind their colleagues of the same generation who, equal in artistic importance, work under similar conditions and in the same atmosphere; as regards the great masters one must not lose sight of their imitators and copyists—and also the forgers.

In itself the 'attributing' of the insignificant works of art does not appear too important; what mainly gets the sublime sport going, and indeed may turn it into a profitable profession, is the insatiable hunger for names on the part of the collectors and dealers. You may do your best by talking to these people and pointing out to them that every work of art, even the poorest one, is due to one human being who has borne a name; and that it depends on accidental circumstances whether the name is known or not. The delusion that something notable clings to each name is ineradicable. Whoever pays a lot of money for a Rembrandt demands to be covered by authoritative judgment. The unconditional respect for names, even obscure ones, is at all events a bad symptom so far as taste and feeling for quality are concerned.

The attention devoted to the lesser masters has proved profitable and fruitful inasmuch as the personalities of the great artists, as a result, have been defined more clearly and decisively. Much has been gained for the understanding of Rembrandt after his pupils and followers, one after the other, have methodically been put on their feet, both biographically and from the point of view of style-criticism. A happy cleansing of his *œuvre* has thus been carried out.

General validity attaches to the maxim that it is easier for the expert to say 'this picture is by such and such a hand' than to gain the conviction that it is *not* by that hand. We judge with greater certainty positively than negatively.

The study of the lesser masters furthers knowledge of the general level, of the style of the period. We learn to know the starting line of the great masters, and see how it is set off lustrously against the dark background of average activity.

XXXI

THE STUDY OF DRAWINGS

NOTHING is to be recommended more strongly to the aspiring connoisseur of pictures, and indeed urged upon him, than assiduous study of drawings. Whoever turns from the pictures of a master to his drawing has the feeling that a curtain rises before him, and that he is penetrating into the inner sanctuary. For more than one reason a drawing is superior to a picture as evidence, as an autograph. It came into being relatively quickly, as a result of spontaneous action, and did not have to take the long and toilsome road through craftsmanlike procedure; it is in consequence less closely tied to teaching, tradition and studio convention. When drawing, the artists of the 15th and 16th centuries were more of artists; when painting, more of craftsmen. The drawing stands in the same relation to painting as a mountain brook to a canal. In many cases the draughtsman is not complying with any wish from outside, does not carry out an order: he feels himself free in mood and fancy, alone with himself, as it were, as speaking a monologue. Moreover, a drawing has hardly ever suffered from

distortion, subsequent alteration, restoration or falsification. Everything lies there open to the day, as at
the moment of its birth.

To draw, in a higher degree than to paint, involves
selection, decision, elimination, spiritual intervention: hence it is inestimable as an immediate, personal, intimate utterance of individuality.

It is regrettable, and a hindrance, that the totality
of surviving drawings should be so very unequally distributed among the centres of art periods and masters.
Scarcely any drawings by Frans Hals and Velazquez
have been traced, and only a few by the great masters
of the 15th century, while, when we come to Raphael,
Leonardo, Dürer and Rembrandt, the number of existing and known drawings is great: indeed, it has im-
measurably enriched the idea of these masters, and in
many respects provided the foundations for it.

In the past the artists stood closer to nature when
they drew than when they painted. The intentions of
the draughtsman were now in this, now in that direction. In many degrees it is a question of attempts,
means of orientation, preparations, models, studies,
designs, gaugings, notations of sudden ideas, ideas of
pictures; but also of self-contained works of art
which were retailed, sought after and collected, like
the coloured drawings of Aelbert Cuyp.

In the course of evolution the drawing freed itself
more and more from painting. At a primitive stage a
picture was nothing but a drawing that had been

coloured, that had been completed by the indication of the local colours. A drawing by Rembrandt differs from a picture by this master more strongly than say a drawing by Roger van der Weyden differs from one of his panel pictures. Painting has gradually realized the specific possibilities given to its means. Drawing, on the other hand, was carried away into the movement, becoming pictorial with richness of tonality and increased looseness of stroke; on the other hand it developed the special style conformable with its means, in the sketch, in the rapid notation, the writing down of the sudden flash of an idea for a picture.

In the highest degree personal, and original in the narrowest sense, are such impressions as we possess by Rembrandt, which mostly bear no relation to pictures, do not exist as auxiliaries or designs, but on the contrary have been done purposelessly, out of the sheer abundance of vision.

As to knowledge of form and the measure of expressive power, the evidence of the drawing is more definite than that of painting, which can conceal shortcomings and cloak defects. Many painters are badly given away by their drawings.

To establish the relationship between drawing and painting in each case is highly instructive. Rubens has utilized studies from nature of individual figures in order to give his painting steadiness and firm structure. In the 15th century the drawing is concealed beneath the layer of colour; it stands in the same relation to painting as the skeleton to the flesh; it is present in painting as something immanent, just as painting is immanent in Rembrandt's drawings.

Fortunately we possess a solidly instructive book in Josef Meder's volume *Die Handzeichnung* (1919), which deals precisely with the art and technique of drawing.

XXXII

INFLUENCE

METAPHORICAL technical terms have the unpleasant quality of being used for many processes or conditions which are different from one another, and eventually also for such as the metaphor does not fit at all. Every effect, which is produced by one master upon another, is called influence. Under the sign of this image we perceive how green waters pour into blue ones, with the result that the colour of the stream is changed. Thereby the idea of a mechanical occurrence is awakened. You should, however, definitely distinguish between occurrences that are mechanical—fundamentally, additions or minglings; chemical reactions; and psychical—the latter so complicated that no term is adequate to their multiplicity. That which is called 'influence' is a psychical occurrence. From case to case, in boundlessly numerous modifications, something occurs—or fails to occur—when two artists or two manners of art collide.

The masters of the past lived in a condition of community, akin to that of the guilds; they worked at times conjointly, and helped each other out. The inclination to segregate oneself, to cultivate individuality as a priceless possession, to isolate oneself, to retire to an island, is connected with the striving for originality characteristic of modern times; while in our days impulses of variegated multiplicity are conveyed to an artist in confusing quantity by exhibitions, museums, photographic reproductions and the teaching of the universities. Ambition causes the modern painter to try to free himself from the eclecticism forced upon him. Tradition was formerly a coercion from which genius alone, and even genius but gradually, freed itself. The painter took over ideas and language of form from his teacher, and felt himself content with his inherited possessions, provided for and armed to perform that which was asked of him. He had what he needed when he made himself independent, and nothing caused him to look out eagerly for impulses and artistic experiences. This was the normal condition of a master who still stood very close to craftsmanship.

Where something can pour in, there a vacuum must exist—in other words, say, an ideal not realized at home or in tradition, ambitious discontent with that which was one's own, a need, a power of attraction. Often the readiness to absorb something foreign was heightened by travels.

With regard to certain masters we are fully informed and are able to measure in detail the effect of the journeys, of the visual experiences abroad. Jan van Scorel, van Dyck and above all Dürer travelled with open eyes, with the wish to learn and to enrich them-

selves. A close examination of individual destinies—
which in the case of Dürer can succeed, especially
thanks to the penetrating analysis of Professor Heinrich Wölfflin—is conducive to conclusions of general
validity.

Dürer and Jan van Scorel lived in a period of thirst
for knowledge, in a restless time, in which the exchange of intellectual possessions and achievements
between the peoples, especially across the Alps, was
longed for and assiduously practised. That which can
be learnt was overvalued—perspective and the theory
of proportion, for instance. Rationalists are more eager
to learn and more capable of learning than naïve people.

In all cases the vessel which receives must first be
examined, and then only the force pouring into it. To
what degree is the vessel empty and in need of content ? Is the master still growing ? Do the forces which
hitherto have nourished him no longer nourish him
sufficiently ? Is the field ploughed and ready to receive
the seed ? These, and similar questions, must be asked
from the fundamental consideration that an artist is
always capable of realizing possibilities that are contained in his disposition whatever he imitates, which-
ever leader he follows, whatever school he passes
through, whatever the track along which he climbs
upwards.

The vessel becomes capable of reception by expel-
ling something. By this I want to say that whoever
acquires something, gives something else away ; he can-

not pile up acquisitions. The adaptable, receptive nature makes sacrifices all the time. It is true that the Academicians in Bologna imagined that they could add or multiply values. Reynolds sought success by composing like Van Dyck and painting like Rembrandt.

The relationship of the forces on the one hand and on the other must be weighed. If a weak talent encounters genius, then it misunderstands although it may give itself up completely; if strong gifts collide with still stronger ones, then there is a possibility of understanding many things, and of robbing the examplar of that which can be utilized.

Compulsion and choice at times stand out in vigorous contrast to one another. Van Dyck laboured in his youth under the terror which issued from Rubens and sacrificed something of his individuality; later in Italy he chose Titian, the Venetian, as a congenial exemplar, and in this fashion freed himself from the Flemish tradition. With the aid of Titian he set personal qualities free, and could now satisfy his desire for *grandezza* and distinction. He was at first like wax which is impressed; then he seized the initiative; finally he combined and became fossilized in routine. Whether it be passive or active, personality reveals itself in all phases also in its capacity to give itself up to something, to disguise itself, to utilize and to blend.

In a similar fashion the relationship of Dürer to Schongauer and to Mantegna should be analysed. The engravings of Schongauer—revealing the manner of

the Late Gothic goldsmith in its highest perfection—
were bound to affect the youthful Dürer as a powerful
magnet. When his own forces burst the narrowness
of this form of style, Mantegna—severe in his greatness and solidly constructive—offered precisely that
which the German artist, conformably with his nature
and his then stage of maturity, could absorb from
Italian art as a nourishment that was wholesome and
favourable to his growth.

Little noted, and yet very notable, is the *absence* of
effect. Bruegel was in Rome and seems to have perceived neither Raphael nor classical statues. The vessel
does not admit not only because it is closed, but also
because it is full. That which was intuitively expected
is welcomed. That which someone loves, respects,
understands, imitates—then, the way in which he misunderstands it, and that which he overlooks—all this
completes in an instructive fashion the idea of a personality. A painter chooses as his leader a master in whose
works he has found his unsubstantial dreams realized.

Some masters were imitated because their method
of painting called forth admiration: but it was the
creators of types, the story-tellers who, stimulating
and affording an example, exercised a much stronger
influence. This influence reached far and wide, especially once the picture-print had intervened as a vehicle
of popularization, conveniently offering, as it were,
an excerpt of the imitable. Masters who have heightened and extended their domination through engrav-

21. HANS HOLBEIN, MADONNA OF THE BURGOMASTER MEYER

Darmstadt, Grand Ducal Castle

1525-26

ing—original and/or reproductive—are Schongauer, Dürer, Raphael, Rubens and Watteau.

The Middle Ages appear cosmopolitan so far as art is concerned, since the world domination of the Church did not allow the individual tendencies of the nations and peoples quite to develop. Just as the scholars of all countries could understand each other by means of Latin, so did the artists express themselves in a language of form which was homogeneous, though rich in vernacular. Later on, as the conception of the world became more mundane, and as the national states emerged, the North separated from the South. Personality, in freeing itself, drew also the characteristics of the race, of the people into the light. Now as the Italians with an unspoilt eye turned to reality, they concentrated themselves with fanatical onesidedness on the human body whose loveliness, strength, dignity and nobility were glorified in proud self-consciousness. In the North, on the other hand, more attention was turned to the human soul, and to the interconnection of body, space, light, and atmosphere.

The accurate and conscientious observation practised by the Netherlandish masters, coupled reciprocally with the detailed method of painting, fixed on the object and invested the entire production with something reminiscent of still life, a comfortable, contemplative narrowness and stiffness. The pictures from the North struck the South as being pious, with ascetic vigour or collected devotion. The successes gained in Italy by the professional landscape painters from the North—such as Paul Bril, Elsheimer, Poussin, Claude—confirm a superiority in this field which was recognized, even if too high a value was not placed on it. Of 'noble' art there was demanded that which the Italians could give with unsurpassable mastery, and therefore Netherlandish, German and French painters in the 16th century went to the foreign school, where they strove to learn picture-building with human bodies in movement as their material. The plants transplanted in the North burst forth in strange flowers.

About 1450 Memling left the Middle Rhine, Schongauer Alsace, Dürer's father, the goldsmith, Hungary—and all for the Netherlands in search of the 'great masters'; but Dürer in 1495 went to Northern Italy. It is profitable to follow the exchange which took place between North and South, of motifs, language of form, artistic knowledge, technical means. In each individual case it is different relationships and different consequences and results which ensue. We must measure capability of reception, readiness, the strength of the innate gifts which are capable of digesting the alien substance. Gossaert, Jan van Scorel, Frans Floris, Rubens, and van Dyck stayed in the South, eager to learn, and in each case analysis proves a different relationship of gain and loss, of nourishment and poison. Rubens provides the image of an unique victory. He avoided no danger of eradication and overcame every one of them; he gave himself up consciously to Italian Baroque, and eventually freed himself from it unconsciously.

The great masters, mighty in their rule and sweeping us along, exercise seductive attraction on their own generation and those that follow, if and as long as they express themselves in harmony with current taste, and remain comprehensible up to a point. In their full maturity they are capable either of taking or of giving. They work then in exalted seclusion and isolation, and their followers, who always misunderstand or caricature a little, desert them. It is the gift of a genius to see things which his contemporaries do not see. The latest works of Rembrandt and Titian have been least imitated. Frans Hals and Rubens, too, attracted more adepts when they began than at the end of their career. Those who ran after them could not keep pace, but lagged behind.

Their achievement and quick push forward mean that the great masters move in advance of their time with such speed, and so far, that the importance of their example is recognized only long after their death. Thus it is, strictly speaking, only in the 19th century that Velazquez has exercised influence, and Frans Hals, at any rate in his late manner, has not been appreciated or imitated at an earlier date either. Goya is in the same position. The case of Greco is somewhat different, since this old master was discovered as an ancestor rather than as a teacher.

XXXIII

ARTISTIC QUALITY: ORIGINAL AND COPY

O N reading—impatiently or with a patient smile —elaborate dissertations which 'prove' that a picture is by such and such a master, at the end we generally, after many arguments and references, come upon the word 'quality'. This means that the decisive point, which also brings things to a dead end, has been reached. You derive the impression that the entire letterpress—lengthy, spasmodic, crowded with quotations—is just counsel's pleading, while the judge who condemns or acquits solely uses the word 'quality'. The concept of 'quality' arrests the flow of words of even the most garrulous.

When an impression fills us with pleasurable satisfaction—with 'disinterested pleasure' as the aestheticians say—it springs from a pure, individual and hence uniform vision and also from a successful realization of this vision, thanks to which the emotional values are communicated to us without any considerable loss. We hear an individually coloured voice which says something that we know, but says it in

22. AFTER HANS HOLBEIN
MADONNA OF THE BURGOMASTER MEYER
Dresden Gallery
Painted about 1632-1638

such a fashion that we think we hear it for the first time.

A pleasurable sensation of a definite degree and a definite kind is, in our experience, associated with the works of this or that master. We stand in expectation of some such kind of delight as a work of art can produce—a sense of elevation, of shock, of revelation, of disclosure, of rapture, or whatever the case may be—and we decide on authorship and authenticity according as such an experience does or does not take place.

The connoisseur of wine determines with full certainty brand and vintage from a particular flavour: in the same way, the connoisseur of art recognizes the author on the strength of the sensually spiritualized impression that he receives. Sometimes it is a question of lovely equipoise, sometimes of stark, exciting vividness, sometimes again of an intensification of the sense of life, or a sense of pathos, of boundless abundance, of heroic exaltation—and every time the accent is unmistakable. Always quality shows itself in this, that emotional values experienced by the artist in his vision are interpreted in visible terms.

I must anticipate the query whether the quality of, say, a still-life or a slight scene from passing life is due to a successful interpretation of spiritual emotion. The answer is, Yes; only it is necessary fully to understand what has happened. When Chardin saw a fruit this visual experience filled him with delicate enjoyment, and this sensation invested eye and hand with the capacity to paint as he did. Again, when Pieter de Hooch painted the roof of a house, so deeply did he feel the marvel of light in the wealth of colours and tonal values, that he was able to communicate to the spectator, in full purity and completeness, the delight, the peaceful pleasure that the world, as he had seen it, had given him.

It is only the line put down at the dictate of feeling, only the brushstroke guided by instinct—nothing that is taught, calculated, selected or painstakingly improved upon—which communicates the vibrations of feeling and thereby that experience for the sake of which art has value to us. No wonder that the differences between good and bad, measured or weighed, appear infinitesimal.

An unsatisfactory column, shall we say, is the one which is drawn as with the ruler. To the good architect the column is an organism with a soul, suffering, triumphant, carrying and burdened; and in the scarcely measurable, delicate life of the outline there are expressed strength, tension, pressure and resistance.

The notion of quality is brought out by a comparison between an original and a copy better than by the best definition. Such a comparison makes us penetrate deep into the essence of artistic production. The understanding of Holbein's art was furthered with quick strides, thanks to the 'Holbein War'—the occasion when, in 1871, the Darmstadt Madonna was placed alongside of the Dresden picture, with the result that the celebrated Dresden version was recognized as a copy dating from the seventeenth century. Adolph Bayersdorfer's brochure *Der Holbein-Streit* (1872) can still be read with profit, even for other aspects of the subject.

All opinions—even the mistaken ones—expressed on the two versions are instructive. You find them reprinted in a publication by G. T. Fechner entitled *Ueber die Echtheitsfrage der Holbein-Madonna* (1871). And, incidentally, a striking demonstration is thus provided of the supremacy of experts with a historical point of view over artists who go by a canon of beauty which belongs to the nineteenth century.

Bayersdorfer—who, in the discussion over the Holbein Madonna at Dresden, formulated the arguments against the authenticity of the picture in the most pointed fashion—described notably the colouring as irreconcilable with the manner of Holbein. At a period of advanced 'pictorial' vision—that is at the beginning of the seventeenth century when the copy was painted—the painters strove after a harmony of colour which entailed the sacrifice of the local colours. Holbein, on the other hand—from the period to which he belonged and particularly from his personal bent—had an objective respect for the local colours, and has never falsified the flesh tints through coloured reflections and greenish half-tints. If it is objected that for once he might have painted differently from his wont, you overlook the fact that end and means, spirit and pictorial technique, form and colour, all having an identical origin, are bound to agree in a given picture; and indeed, in the Darmstadt original the discrepancies, patent to every sensitive eye at Dresden, are in no wise to be traced. If, however, many amateurs and artists about 1870 found the Dresden picture 'more beautiful' than the Darmstadt one, this verdict of taste is to be explained through the fact that those judges, as regards their visual convention, were still closer to the time about 1630 than to the time about 1530.

The copyist, by contrast to the creative master, takes as his starting point a picture, not life; and is concerned with a vision already realized. In a way, of course, there exists no such thing as absolutely original production. Strictly speaking it is a question of difference of degrees. Even a great and independent painter has not only seen nature but also works of art, paintings by other masters and his own. He depends upon a tradition of art. To some extent every painter is an imitator and copyist, if only in this, that he paints his picture from his own nature studies, drawings, sketches. In the professional routine no one can escape recollection of the work of others and of his own earlier work. The artist in fact is not only father and mother to his production, but also the *accoucheur*.

We might endeavour to set out a synopsis of degrees. As works to be classified as original in the

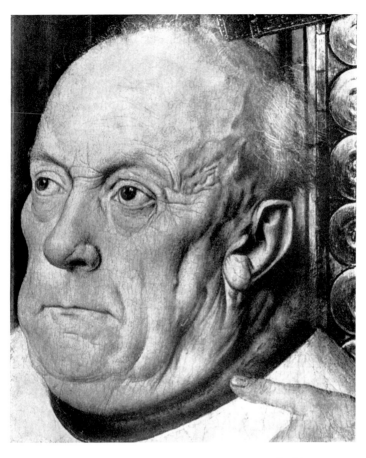

23. JAN VAN EYCK, CANON VAN DER PAELE
Detail of the Altarpiece in the Bruges Museum

highest degree you might put down, say, drawings by Rembrandt—notably those of his late period—or drawings by Grünewald. By their very nature, drawings rank higher than paintings in the table of precedence we are now establishing. Directness and spontaneity are indissolubly linked with originality. The lowest rank is that of copies in the narrow and rigorous sense of the word. And there are endless quantities of intermediate stages.

The truly creative master struggles with the task of projecting on the picture surface the vision which exists in his imagination. He can approach his goal but never reach it, and herein lies the stimulating, exciting fascination of his activity—and also, to be sure, the tragedy of his destiny. The copyist faces a task which is laborious and soporific but, in his view, perfectly feasible. Before his eyes he has the artist's projection, which constitutes the real task, and he requires only keenness of perception and skill in order to perform his work.

Whoever copies need not be incapable of independent creation. It is even conceivable that the artist in question may be more highly gifted than he who produced the archetype. The decisive point is, however, that the servitude and duty of the copyist's task stamp his performance with the character of subordination and lack of freedom; that his mental attitude, whoever he be, is essentially different from that of the creative artist. As soon as he copies the painter renounces his own method of vision. The creative master stakes the whole of his intellectual and spiritual forces, the copyist only memory, eye and hand. Whoever feels the difference between growing and making is not going to be easily deceived. An original resembles an organism; a copy, a machine.

Generally the decisive hall-mark of an original is the perfect harmony it establishes between pictorial imagination and form, between conception and execution, between formative intention and the means of expression. An original is in harmony with itself. The further in time a copyist is parted from the production of the archetype, the less is he capable of reaching this homogeneousness—or even of mimicking it—since, even if he were able completely to suppress his method of vision, he lacks the pigments and mediums which went to produce the original.

Now there do, of course, exist contemporary copies, and workshop replicas. With regard to these, the decision is often difficult. Even the ambiguous, evasive expression 'replica', to which experts often resort from uncertainty or may be politeness—suggests the possibility of producing a perfectly successful facsimile. Even assuming that a master has, with his own hand, copied one of his works (usually such tasks were no doubt allotted to his assistants) it is to be expected that he would be unable in the repetition to reach the freshness and vitality of the first creation. It is true that masters such as Gerard Dou and Gerard Terborch, who work with phlegmatic accomplishment, methodically and coolly, probably do not betray themselves as copyists of their own works.

Copies have been, and are being, commissioned and produced with motives and intentions that are different from one another. Academic training through the imitation of classical masterpieces; the desire to retain the duplicate of a sold picture—such cases entail the striving after accurate reproduction and the complete effect of the archetype.

At times independent masters have produced paraphrases of older works without suppressing their own manner of expression, as for instance Delacroix when he translated Rubens into his own language of art. And Rubens acted similarly—even if not so consciously—when he paraphrased pictures by Titian. The conflict, inevitable in these cases, between conception and pictorial treatment results in ambiguous or hybrid effects. Formerly copies were frequently made light-heartedly, without the ambition to approach the archetype, notably in order to put on record a composition, to make a reproduction, before the invention of photography. In such cases it is easy to convince oneself that the master concerned cannot be credited with the invention of the work. We feel at once that we have before us a corrupted, poorly interpreted text.

As for the faithful, excellent and successful copies —and only these are disturbing to style-criticism, notably if the archetypes are unknown or not available for comparison—there are some general considerations which will help us to avoid mistakes.

Copying is a business which calls for feminine devotion, readiness for sacrifice, patient and never failing attention. Copies often are slower in coming into being than originals. It is hardly to be avoided that eye and hand grow tired at the wearisome task, that everything does not succeed uniformly. And it is to be expected that the copyist concentrates his undistracted attention preferably upon the essential passages, which are of decisive importance for the total effect, and, on the other hand, devotes less care to trifling details. If it is a question of a Madonna, he will be more sympathetic, take more time and trouble, when painting the head of the Virgin than when dealing with the landscape background or the ornaments of the architectural setting. Relaxing and waning of accuracy are not infrequently to be observed in the corners or along the edges of the copy.

A second consideration seems to contradict the first one. I remember in this connection a conference which I attended at the Government Printing Office in Berlin. A decision was to be taken regarding new currency notes. An art lover on the Committee made an eloquent plea for sacrificing the portraits—admittedly mostly lacking in taste—in favour of purely ornamental designs. At this the representative of the Reichsbank protested energetically. Precisely the por-

By gracious permission of His Majesty The King

24. AFTER JAN VAN EYCK, CANON VAN DER PAELE

Hampton Court Palace

trait heads, he urged, were indispensable, a part of the picture on no account to be left out. This was because it had been noticed that the Bank cashiers, who quickly had to make up their mind as to the genuineness of notes, instinctively looked first at the head, the expression of the face, and reached their decision accordingly. I have never forgotten this experience from the practical domain of detection.

For it is a fact: a tiny alteration of the ensemble of forms—scarcely measurable, nay, so small that a copyist or forger hardly can avoid it—brings about in the face and notably round the mouth a considerable, immediately apprehended variation of spiritual expression. An equally slight alteration of an ornamental design is scarcely capable of proof, and in any case not noticeable at first glance.

The portrait need be no masterpiece, yet in every case the psyche of a human being impresses itself upon the cashier who has seen thousands of notes; and the character image, now so familiar, is immediately missed by him in the forged notes.

The expert reacts in no way differently from this bank cashier. There exist accomplished copies of engravings before which one glance at a human face saves you from error more certainly than the most painstaking comparison of other parts of the plate.

The copyist is least successful when striving after the interpretation of spiritual expression; and when it is a matter of accessories, his eagerness flags.

ARTISTIC QUALITY: ORIGINAL AND COPY

I have already noted that drawings tell you more about the essence of original work than pictures. Hence, when we study drawings, the fundamental difference between archetype and copy becomes most easily apprehended. Graphology can teach us much about the difference between true-born and imitated form. The copyist draws warily, directing his eye alternately at his exemplar and the copy, and is even for this reason incapable of achieving the boldly flowing sweep of the archetype.

Even the best copyist cannot avoid misunderstandings. The master who works direct from nature and realizes his own vision, has taken in much more than he notes down—what he gives is an excerpt, a shorthand note, an abbreviation. He may indicate, say, the contour of a hat with a slight stroke of the pen; but he has seen and knows the building up of the other side and the interior of the piece of head-gear, as also the material it is made of. Something of this expert knowledge guided his hand as he drew the contour. The copyist has before his eyes the result of a visual action in which he takes no part. A tiny projection or twist of the original line has a cause which the copyist does not know, a significance of which he is ignorant.

I will try to illustrate by means of an example the kind of mistake which a copyist is liable to make. Before me there lie two drawings, one the archetype, the other a close imitation. In the foreground, out of the earth, there rises a stone across whose base there

extends a wavy mass of sand. The copyist has erroneously taken the slight, undulating line for the lower
edge of the stone, which now in the copy is not contained in the soil but, on the contrary, stands *on* the
ground with an impossible jagged contour. The ensemble of forms seems in each case to be almost
exactly the same, yet the total effect is completely
different, since the copy has wiped out the special
illusion caused by the position of the stone behind the
wavy mass of sand.

Silhouettes which overlap, foreshortenings and
concealments of forms, are means of suggesting the
third dimension on the flat surface. Since the copyist,
unlike the creative draughtsman, has not seen the
volumes in space he is incapable of understanding
more especially those lines which take us in the direction of depth. If an outline collides with an outline in
a different direction, if such an outline is cut through,
then form becomes partly concealed, turning from
the picture-space towards the depth. Three-dimensional appearance, cubic mass and the movement of a
body in space are conjured up by insignificant con-
tractions, interruptions, and the end and beginning
of the stroke of the pen. There is marvellous vitality
in the intermittent handling of Leonardo's sketchy
drawings, which nobody can copy without neutral-
izing the *staccato* or else—if the imitation be mechani-
cally cautious—without losing the suggestive effect.
In considering gaps and omissions, say, in Rem-

brandt's drawings, it is to be borne in mind that the master drew for himself and that completeness did not come within his intentions. Such forms as adjoin the gaps must give the spectator the possibility of building bridges in his imagination. To the extent that the connection is not provided, it must be created. A drawing by Leonardo or Rembrandt, as outcome of a vision, is for the spectator nothing but a means to let that vision revive. The examination is an experiment aimed at establishing whether this ensemble of strokes and dots produces the vision. Truly it is not a slight performance which in this fashion is demanded of the judge.

The hall-mark of originality is the individual character which is peculiar to the work and all its component parts; in a manner of speaking, the resemblance to the creator of that which is created. Now there also exists an originality of inferior rank; one that has been *made*, alongside of the one which has grown naturally. Especially at a time when native strength and personal individuality are held in high esteem as being of basic importance for the true artist, it is the desire of everyone who handles brush and pencil to be himself an original, and when, as is so often the case, the necessary resources are insufficient, the person concerned wilfully resorts to that which is bizarre; and to differentiate this from that which is original is far from easy and, indeed, frequently impracticable for contemporaries. Something original is strange when first seen, shocking and unpleasant; something bizarre is striking and entertaining. The former is something enduring and permanent and only gains in impressiveness; the latter is a thing of fashion, is ephemeral, causes satiety and vanishes before long. The relation of original to bizarre is that of the man of genius to the *fantaisiste*. Whoever is creative in a truly original sense—especially if he be a man of genius— aims at being self-sufficient; whoever indulges in the bizarre, endeavours to impress his contemporaries or to amaze them.

We often hesitate to use the derogatory word 'copy' and look in vain for another term. In periods of strictly binding iconographical tradition—in the middle ages and as late as the fifteenth century—compositions and pictorial motifs were repeated, without any intention of achieving an artistic effect. 'What', not 'How', was the important thing, and it was far from rare that refinement, animation, happy re-arrangement of a traditional pictorial idea, were realized at a later stage. A free translation into a new language was given of the text. More particularly icon-like, hieratic images enjoyed a long lease of life, re-tained their standing for reasons which had little to do with artistic value. At times there may have attached to them the prestige of special sanctity or miraculous powers; and they may for that reason over and over again have been welcome and desirable to the pious.

In order to gain the correct standpoint in regard to

such phenomena, we must free ourselves from certain prejudices. The concept of the 'artist', with his jealous claim on intellectual ownership, came gradually into being from the sixteenth century onwards. Previously, it was a matter of illustrating the story of the Gospels and the Legends for the benefit of the faithful, and of making the saintly character tangible. The situations could only be understood, and the persons recognized, if they were to be seen in familiar guise. Owing to the need of making himself understood, the artist's possibilities of expression were restrained and limited. Neither the painter nor the community had ever seen St. Peter, but they knew pictures of him. Illusion and vague belief connected such images with archetypes, which reached back to the period of the saint. Veneration was extended to authentic, true portraits of the Saviour and to Madonna pictures which St. Luke, as was thought, had painted from life.

If one realizes the spiritual relationship of the pious to the devotional image, then one no longer wonders at the faithfulness to tradition which, taking medieval iconography as its starting-point, kept alive compositions, motifs and types. There were times when the new pictorial conception could not count on understanding, indeed was regarded as blasphemous. In all probability Jan van Eyck, Hugo van der Goes and Grünewald did not only satisfy but also disturb their contemporaries. No doubt, bearing this in mind, the

25. BRUGES MASTER OF 1499, MADONNA WITH DONORS
Paris, Louvre
The composition in part goes back to Hugo van der Goes

breaking down of the pious convention through masters of genius appears all the more worthy of admiration. Originality was neither asked for nor encouraged; on the contrary it had to overcome strong resistance.

XXXIV

DEDUCTIONS 'A POSTERIORI' FROM COPIES REGARDING LOST ORIGINALS

OUR heritage of works by the Old Masters shows
many gaps. Destructive action has, in the course
of centuries, intervened more radically in one place
than in another. Italian art cities, like Florence or
Siena, had in essentials remained untouched until the
greed and eagerness of collectors and dealers not indeed destroyed but carried off the artists' works.
North of the Alps, on the other hand, icono-
clastic movements, wars and revolutions have made
terrible ravages; nor have they halted before ecclesiastical property, which in the South has remained relatively unharmed. Some countries, districts and
cities have been looted almost down to the last vestige, for example France and Holland, and certain
German cities like Ulm and Augsburg. If style-
criticism has been successful in assembling and classi-
fying at any rate a modest remnant of Dutch panel
painting of the 15th century, this is due to the fact
that a few examples, more particularly of small
dimensions, were sent out of the country and thus
saved from falling into the hands of the iconoclasts.

THE ARCHAEOLOGICAL METHOD

In the case of the great Flemish and Dutch masters of the 15th century we possess only a fraction of that which originally existed of their production. Many works mentioned in records or in old writings can no longer be traced.

Since there was much copying and imitation going on in the Netherlands—as I have described, and in the spirit that I have indicated—we must conclude that there exist copies that do not automatically reveal themselves as such precisely because the archetypes are lost; and their number is greater than is generally supposed.

We turn for instruction to the archaeologists, whose efforts, when based on style-criticism, are almost exclusively directed towards deducing lost originals from copies, towards the reconstructing of the archetype from one or more imitations. Thus to transfer the method, perfected by the archaeologists, into the study of 15th century painting has occasionally been productive of valuable results. The analysing eye sees through the disfiguring garments with which the master in charge of the immediate execution has cloaked the body of the archetype.

In each case questions such as these should be asked: 'Is the artist to whom we owe the execution also the one whom we may credit with the invention? Does the manner of painting, chronologically and as regards artistic value, accord with the conception? Can we notice, within the composition, a contradiction, a break, a sudden transition, a lack of logic? Do the parts fit in with each other and the whole? A negative answer to these questions, or to one of them, justifies the deduction 'copy' or 'free copy'—that is, a mixture of copy and independent work. We aim at discovering the author of the archetype and, in so far as Flemish 15th century is concerned, we can restrict our search to a relatively small circle, since experience has taught us that, as creators of types, there are but few masters to be considered, namely, Jan van Eyck, Roger van der Weyden, Dirk Bouts, Hugo van der Goes and Jerome Bosch.

I will try to illustrate by one example how such an investigation can be carried out successfully.

In the Louvre there is a Madonna picture which has achieved undeserved fame because a French scholar, on the basis of the initials J. P., claimed it for Jean Perréal. This idea was mistaken. The initials relate to the couple shown as donors. The picture is Flemish, painted about 1500—the costume also tells us that—and it is by an unimportant painter, whose petty manner may be recognized in some other panels.

The Madonna sits enthroned in the middle; the male and the female donor are shown as half-lengths on the left and right behind the sides of the throne. If anything has been created independently by the painter, then it is the couple of donors who gave him the commission. Now it is the portraits which are the weakest part of the whole; they enable us to measure a spiritual narrowness, which also reveals itself in the dry and pedantic elaboration of the decoration of the metal throne and of the piece of brocade. The face of the Madonna is empty and inexpressive—possibly 'beautified' by a restorer. On the other hand in the play of folds in the Madonna's garments, and in the Infant Christ with its vigorous movement, will and temperament are active as expressive forces which lie beyond the possibilities of the painter to whom the execution is due. The tubes and ridges of the drapery, boldly crossing, and colliding with, each other; a dramatic and imaginative language of form, in a poor translation it is true, point to Hugo van der Goes. The Infant Christ, lying across the lap of His Mother and raising the upper part of the body, partakes—in the face, in the movement of the lean body, and in the fingers, spasmodically bent inwards—of the emotional life of the Ghent master, with its intense yearning. The motif of movement does not seem to be fully justified or consistent in this context. One does not see who or what has caught the attention of the Child and caused its action. The motif is borrowed, taken out of a different connection. Probably there were in the archetype female saints close to the Madonna, and the Child turned vivaciously to one of the saints, perhaps St. Catherine.

We may hence insert, as a welcome increment, some parts of this inconsiderable picture into our idea of the activity of Hugo van der Goes.

XXXV

WORKSHOP PRODUCTION

A PICTURE is, in accordance with the view which nowadays has acquired general validity, the creation of one single person, who was the only one working at it from its conception down to the last brush-stroke and who is held to be solely responsible for it. It is with difficulty that we accustom ourselves to note, and to draw deductions from the fact, that this was not always so. The painters of bygone days were at the head of a workshop; they worked together with journeymen and apprentices. Now this circumstance is, it is true, occasionally taken into account by style-criticism, and the derogatory term 'workshop production' is introduced—especially in cases where an original can be compared with a weaker replica which is nevertheless identical in composition and pictorial technique. Without a doubt collaboration was far-reaching, and is not restricted to the cases in which the dissatisfied eye looks in vain for the expected quality, or can establish an inequality of merit in the pictorial execution. 'Autograph' quality is questionable also in cases where the defects of execution are by no means patent. Gifted journeymen

26. LUCAS CRANACH, PORTRAIT OF PHILIP OF POMERANIA

Rheims, Museum

A record from life

and even boy apprentices may, as regards ability, have been equal, and even superior, to the head of the workshop. It is to be borne in mind that a journey-man did not, as an Academy student does nowadays, create himself a master the moment he imagined he had learnt enough; on the contrary, economic conditions might cause him to persevere as an assistant, all the more so as the master had an interest in keeping skilled collaborators.

Jan van Scorel was, as regards artistic gifts, at least a match for his third master, the Amsterdam painter Jacob Cornelisz. At the age of about twenty-four he received from Jacob, for 'ingenious and skilful' work, a certain sum of money and, in addition, permission to paint in his free time some pictures for himself. This Karel van Mander tells us. It is scarcely to be as-sumed that Jan van Scorel's collaboration lowered the value of the pictures which about 1520 issued from this Amsterdam workshop. One would rather deduce that they showed a less stiff and rejuvenated manner. And it is necessary to reckon with similar conditions also elsewhere

Agreements, whose texts still exist, throw a vivid light on the methods of work which were customary in the studios of the 15th and 16th century. Particu-larly notable is the lawsuit about an altarpiece that Albert Cornelisz. was to supply about 1520. In the agreement with the people at Bruges who had or-dered the picture, it was stipulated that the master was to paint everything essential—especially the flesh —with his own hand. Since this was laid down by agreement we may conclude that even partially 'autograph' quality was not supposed to be a matter of course, that Albert Cornelisz. in other cases did not at all intervene with his handiwork, but contented himself with providing the preparatory drawing and supervising the work. And up to a point such a procedure may have been general in the Flemish workshops of the 16th century. Things do not seem to have been very different in Venice, say in the studio of Giovanni Bellini. Of the lawsuit at Bruges I have spoken at length in the twelfth volume of my *Geschichte der Altniederländischen Malerei*, on the basis of the document published by the late Mr. Weale. Many masters were something akin to owners of business-concerns, or heads of factories.

Frans Floris was, about 1550, the leading master in Antwerp, and an organizer like Rubens half-a-century later. As Karel van Mander relates, one counted one hundred and twenty painters who had learnt and worked under him. Very informative as regards the way in which things were run here are further statements by the same writer. Floris made the preparatory drawing of the composition with chalk, and then let his journeymen do the underpainting and 'continue'; he would tell them to 'bring in these heads in such and such a place'. The fact is that he kept in the workshop, as models and exemplars, a number of

27. WORKSHOP OF LUCAS CRANACH, PORTRAIT OF PHILIP OF POMERANIA

studies of heads which he himself had painted on wood. Such studies by Floris have survived in considerable numbers. Nobody took any exception to this procedure, and Karel van Mander records with praise that, as a result, the pupils achieved sureness and independence.

Completely 'autograph' quality was the exception. Even Dürer, so conscious of his duty and conscientious, stresses in his letters to Heller as something extraordinary that he had let no apprentice take a hand at his work, and hints that he used to execute 'ordinary pictures' (*gemein gemäl*), which paid him better, with the assistance of pupils.

The boy apprentices were there not only to learn; they were also auxiliaries, who were compensated with food and lodging for their performance. They bound themselves to serve for many years, and the master was entitled to hope that as years went by they would prove increasingly useful. After all it was impossible that year after year they should all day long grind colours, clean brushes and perform other menial services; on the contrary, they must have taken some part in the actual painting. They could not possibly learn how to paint without painting.

As to the running of the workshop of Rubens, we are well informed. The letters of the master contain certain passages which tell us a lot. In the year 1619 Rubens writes to William, Duke of Neuburg: 'The *St. Michael* is a difficult subject. I fear that I shall have difficulty in finding among my pupils someone who will be capable of executing the work, even if I provide the drawing. In any case it will be necessary for me to retouch the work with my own hand.' The picture is in the Alte Pinakothek at Munich.

The superiority of genius, its inimitability, will naturally become patent to sensitive eyes. Rubens, especially late in life, painted pictures which in every sense are 'autograph'. Style-criticism can in this case attempt with some confidence to draw the boundary lines of workshop performance and the intervention of a collaborator as gifted as Van Dyck.

So far as medium masters are concerned, it is only the part of incapable and perhaps self-willed apprentices that can be segregated: skilful, well-trained ones remain concealed. If I describe a picture as a work by Bernard van Orley I am, strictly speaking, stating no more than that the master has made his style clearly and uniformly visible, despite a collaboration—not to be checked—by capable apprentices.

A painter who for financial reasons increases the production of his workshop—Lucas Cranach in his Wittenberg period offers an instructive example—does not so much raise the apprentices to his own level: rather, he descends to theirs; he creates a language of form and manner of painting which can be taught and imitated, and gives his production an impersonal character.

It is extremely instructive to compare the surviving

28. HANS CRANACH, PORTRAIT OF A MAN
Lugano, Castle Rohoncz Collection
Signed and dated 1534 H C

'autograph' portrait studies by Cranach, notably those in the Museum at Rheims, with the pictures as executed. They were put to the same use as the 'heads' in the Floris studio. The master seized upon the essentials of the individual face by means of the draughtsman's shorthand. His recordings give pleasure through their striking unambiguousness and are lacking in detail. It is obvious that the master thought of the purpose, of the usableness, of the exemplars and wished to give the apprentices definite and unmistakable directions. In the pictures as executed—their relation to the recordings is that of copies—the scheme is not in the least enriched, and the simplicity after the manner of the woodcut strikes one, when taken over into painting, as empty and rigid.

If we disregard the portraits, copying in the strict sense of the word was not practised in the workshop of Cranach. Obviously the master felt responsible for the composition, regarded it as a matter of honour to provide variants. What we see is over and over again the *Judgment of Paris*, similarly conceived, similarly painted with the same types, but with varied grouping and changed motifs of movement. The *Maître des demi-figures* proceeded in the same way, while Joos van Cleve, the Master of Frankfurt, and other Netherlandish painters caused more or less accurate copies to be made in the workshop. It would be utterly mistaken to deduce 'autograph' execution from the principle of variation, pedantically clung to in the Cranach workshop.

255

It has not proved possible to differentiate, in the later work of Cranach, between him and his sons. Attempts were, indeed, made to segregate the part taken by the elder son, Hans; but these had to be abandoned after the discovery of two panels, signed by Hans Cranach, which as regards style mark no difference from the homogeneous mass of pictures which about 1535 issued from the father's workshop. Both pictures are now in the Castle Rohoncz collection at Lugano.

Netherlandish altarpieces with wings, and devotional pictures, which especially in Antwerp were produced in very large numbers for the market and for the export trade, were not infrequently elsewhere, more particularly at Cologne and Bruges, supplied with portraits of the donors. There exist Flemish wings of altarpieces with portraits by Barthel Bruyn, and others in the style of the Antwerp Mannerists with likenesses by the master known as Adriaen Ysenbrant.

A salutary education towards scepticism and doubt is experienced in studying the inventories published by J. Denucé.[1] One gets scared by the multitude of painters' names with which we cannot link any conception of style; also by the large number of pictures which are put down as copies.

The critic of style must frequently expect that joint work by many painters which has become so alien to

[1] J. Denucé, *De Antwerpsche 'Konstkamers'* (The Hague, 1932).

29. STYLE OF THE ANTWERP MANNERISTS
WINGS OF AN ALTARPIECE
London Art Market
The portrait of the donor inserted by Adriaen Ysenbrant

us. Joachim Buecklaer painted the clothes in portraits by Antonio Moro. This is stated by Karel van
Mander. Houbraken, in speaking of Kneller, remarks,
probably with some exaggeration, that it was the general rule in England for the master to paint only the
face and hands, while the clothes and subsidiary details were painted by others.

XXXVI

ON FORGERIES

MANY of the principles which I have outlined when treating of copies apply also to forgeries, only that the intention to deceive causes an ethical discord to penetrate into the domain of aesthetics, and that a cunning, stealthy attitude of mind replaces the circumspectly and honestly plodding one of the copyist. In face of the disguise, the affectation and hypocrisy which defile art, the connoisseur becomes a criminologist.

At the leading string of a master the forger moves most nearly with security and achieves his aim most easily by copying. In so doing he runs, however, the risk of being caught out, as the archetype generally is known, and a glance at it threatens to expose the fraud. For this reason experienced and ingenious forgers aim at extracting from several archetypes an apparently new whole. In putting together heterogeneous parts they give themselves away. They will imitate, say, the 15th century manner of painting, but will choose a motif of movement characteristic of the 16th century; or they place a headgear of the 16th century on a cranium with a coiffure of the 15th century. Con-

30. HANS HOLBEIN, PORTRAIT OF A MAN
Drawing. Royal Library, Windsor

31. PORTRAIT OF A MAN
Forgery based on the Holbein drawing, reproduced Plate 30

fusion of styles and disharmony are typical of a forgery even more than of a copy. Homogeneousness from the moment of its birth—the hall mark of originality—is lacking.

The forger will copy, closely and cleverly, a Holbein drawing; in the reverse, moreover, so as thereby also to cover up his traces a little. The beard and coiffure of a given male head denotes the time about 1530. The forger places on it a tall cap, of the kind that was worn about 1490, and adds a landscape background in the style of Memling.

The forger is an impostor and a child of his time, who disowns the method of vision which is natural to him. Once the consequences of this disastrous position are clearly realized there will be no difficulty in perceiving the characteristics by which his concoction differs from an original. Oscillating between uneasy cautiousness and brazenness, afraid lest his own voice may grow too loud and betray him, he succumbs to the prejudices of taste that belong to his own period the moment he will give 'beauty'. His pathos sounds hollow, theatrical and forced, since it does not spring from emotion.

The greatest difficulty which besets the forger is that of achieving the decisiveness of the original work —a decisiveness which springs precisely from that naïveté and certainty of instinct which the forger lacks. Deliberation and consciousness reveal themselves in artistic form as lack of life or else hesitation.

The style of the forger's period betrays itself in the expression often through sentimentality, sweetness, a desire to please and insipidness. The forger differs from the master, into whose skin he slips, also in this, that he has but an inadequate knowledge of the object that the master in question had before his eyes. He does not know how a coat was cut and sewn in the 15th century. From our archaeological knowledge we are in a position to discover his mistake and unmask him easily, especially if he has not copied closely but has dared to vary.

The aristocrats among the forgers, a Bastianini or a Dossena, did not strictly speaking work by copying or combining; on the contrary, they harboured the illusion that they had penetrated so deeply into the creative methods of previous ages, that they could express themselves in the spirit, and in the style, of the Old Masters. They dared to push forward, from a 'platonic' production—of which also a gifted connoisseur is capable—into the real one. Success was granted them only for a brief while. They took in only their contemporaries, and even these not permanently. Their works partake of none of that timid pettiness which is characteristic of ordinary forgeries: on the contrary, they display boastfully an audacity which, on their becoming unmasked, transforms itself into foolhardiness.

Since every epoch acquires fresh eyes, Donatello in 1930 looks different from what he did in 1870. That

ÆTATIS · SVÆ · 54

32. HANS HOLBEIN, PORTRAIT OF (?) ANTOINE, DUKE OF LORRAINE
Berlin, Picture Gallery

ANNO·DÑI·1541· · ETATIS·SVÆ·28·

33. HANS HOLBEIN, PORTRAIT OF A MAN
Vienna, Picture Gallery
1541

34. PORTRAIT OF A MAN
*Forgery based on the Holbein portrait at Berlin, Plate 32, but utilizing
the hands in the Vienna portrait by the same master, Plate 33*

which is worthy of imitation appears different to each generation. Hence, whoever in 1870 successfully produced works by Donatello, will find his performance no longer passing muster with the experts in 1930. We laugh at the mistakes of our fathers, as our descendants will laugh at us.

If only for this reason—not to speak of other considerations—it was a silly business when, towards the end of 1908, the Cologne *Madonna with the Sweet Pea* was declared to be a work of the early nineteenth century. I wrote at the time a brief article against this aspersion, and formulated in it the phrase: Forgeries must be served hot, as they come out of the oven. As the 'No' man imagines that he stands above the 'Yes' man—and probably also to others seems to stand higher —critics will always feel the impulse to attack genuine works in order to win the applause of the maliciously minded. The 'Yes' men have done more harm, but have also been of greater usefulness, than the rigorous 'No' men, who deserve no confidence if they never have proved their worth as 'Yes' men.

After being unmasked every forgery is a useless, hybrid and miserable thing. Bastianini was perhaps a talented sculptor; in the style of the past he was, however, only able to bring abortions to the world.

Discussions and polemics regarding forgeries are seldom of long duration. This is the typical sequence of events: the work emerges from obscurity, is admired, then seen through, condemned, and finally sinks into limbo. Behind it are left nothing but silent shame among those that were concerned in the episode, and superior smirks among those not so concerned.

A forgery done by a contemporary is not infrequently successful from being pleasant and plausible, precisely because something in it responds to our natural habit of vision; because the forger has understood, and misunderstood, the old master in the same way as ourselves. Here is, say, a 'Jan van Eyck'—thus the great venerable name, and yet something that has attractiveness in conformity with the taste linked up with our own time: how could it fail to gain applause under such circumstances? To many lovers of art a false Memling is the first Memling that gave pleasure.

I remember how, years ago, an art dealer submitted to me drawings after Holbein's *Dance of Death*, claiming them as originals from the master's hand and referring to the fact that pathos and emotional expression made a stronger appeal in the drawings than in the woodcuts. The observation was accurate; the drawings were, however, imitations of recent date. Holbein, in the woodcut, in the design upon a small scale, has made the motifs of movement—not the facial features—the vehicle of expression: and in this he followed the sure sense of style characteristic of him. The copyist took as his starting-point neither vision nor the requirements of the woodcut, but the intellectual significance of the tragic theme; and, by

35. PORTRAIT OF A MAN
Forgery based on the head of Canon van der Paele, Plate 23

petty strokes of the pen, he heightened the expression of fear and distress in the heads.

Above all things I would not wish that my argument produced the impression that I feel sure of myself. This is by no means the case. Not only I, but also my teachers—for whom I have the greatest regard—have been taken in—though in truth, it seemed impossible to understand, later on, how this had come about.

The eye sleeps until the spirit awakes it with a question. And the question 'Is this work ancient or not?' will at times not be asked, especially not when a dealer deserving of confidence submits the object with the power of suggestion springing from a good conscience and a demand for a high price.

Novel forgeries tend to be most immediately successful. It is easier to deduce from certain characteristics 'This is the work of the forger I know' than to argue negatively 'This cannot be genuine'. In order to give pictures the look of age, the forgers imitate the cracks of the stratum of colour, and this all the more keenly since the wrinkles in the skin of the picture are noted by less gifted amateurs as the only indications of age and genuineness. There exist many genuine pictures which show no cracks, but these are never absent in false ones. The *craquelure* caused by age differs more or less clearly from the one achieved artificially. The primitive method of making cracks by drawing or scratching with pencil or brush is held in contempt by the forgers of our days. It is customary to resort to the trick of producing false cracks by a chemical action —say by sudden heating which causes a coating and breaks up the colour surface lattice-fashion.

The natural cracks penetrate into the gesso preparation, while the artificial ones reach no farther than the colour surface. The imitation, howsoever brought about, lacks the capricious playfulness and irregularity of the network which has come into being gradually and under the influence of climate. The appearance changes according to the character of the pigments and the greater or smaller body of the impasto of colour. In one and the same surface of colour, the cracks will now be very noticeable, now not at all or very faintly discernible.

Accomplished forgers make successful use of old pictures, which they clean radically—often down to the gesso preparation—in order subsequently to superpose their forgery, glazing carefully and treating with the utmost delicacy the *craquelure*, which they leave exposed. The connoisseur is in such cases thrown back upon his sense of style, since the examination of pigments does not help him.

Genuine old pictures are made more valuable through forged signatures. It is, naturally, more convenient and hopeful to supply a good picture by Jan van Kessel with a Ruisdael signature, than to produce a picture by Ruisdael. Signatures of obscure masters have often been cleaned off.

FALSIFICATION

More danger has come to attach to the falsification
—a defiling of works of art which is difficult to combat—than to the forgery in the strict sense of the
word. Let us say that a dealer possesses a Dutch
17th century landscape which has suffered greatly.
From certain indications he considers it—though
wrongly—to be a work by Hercules Seghers, all the
more gladly as the works by this master are scarce and
valuable. He hands the picture over to an able restorer, supervises its cleaning, and supplies reproductions of genuine works in support of his attribution and in order to instruct the restorer. The latter,
without any evil intention, is thus inspired to re-inter-
pret certain passages in the picture 'in the style of
Seghers'. Under the delusion that he has in front of
him a work by the master, he restores it. By slow degrees, proceeding from case to case, the *bona fide* restoration approaches the malevolent falsification. At
times pictures in poor condition have been shown to
me. Of one such I will have said for instance: 'This is
in the manner of Holbein'. And before long it was
once again submitted to me, neatly completed and
with beautiful clearness showing the style of Holbein.

A picture by Vermeer is something exceptionally
precious. Of this master the dealers are dreaming. As
regards their conception, his works do not differ over-
much from those of other and much smaller masters;
the magic of light, colour and the individual technique
of dots give his pictures their singularly exceptional

quality and value. More than once has it happened that modest Dutch landscapes and scenes from daily life have been worked over in an attempt to give them, through vivifying dots of light, the appearance of Vermeer's unique handling of the brush. Tame Dutch pictures have often, by the addition of bold brush strokes, been falsified into works by Frans Hals.

As the forgers, in conformity with their view of their activities, are manufacturers they often produce several versions of a fake: and it may be particularly noted that duplicates have emerged from the Belgian workshops which, during the last few decades, have abundantly seen to the supply of early Netherlandish panels. Machines are identical, while organisms resemble each other.

36. PORTRAIT OF A MAN
Forgery in imitation of Antonello da Messina

XXXVII

ON RESTORATIONS

THE business of the restorer is the most thankless one imaginable. At best one sees and knows nothing of him. If, out of his own invention, he has provided something good he has got mixed up with the dubious company of the forgers; and with the despised one of the destroyers of art if what he has done is bad. His accomplishment remains out of sight, his deficiency leaps to the eye. Judgment regarding the performance of the restorers is even more unreliable than that regarding works of art. And that is saying something.

Restoration is a necessary evil; necessary, inasmuch as threatening decay can be stopped by the laying down of blisters, stabilization of the pigments, strengthening of the ground that carries everything. Moreover artistic value can be increased through cleaning, through the removal of later disfigurements, of retouches and of varnish, darkened or even ruined and gone opaque. Thirdly—and here the intervention begins to become of doubtful value—the restorer supplements, fills in holes, from a delusion of being able to re-establish the original condition.

Even the purely preserving action is accompanied by risk. The old canvas has, say, decayed; so new material is glued to the reverse of the old one. This entails ironing, not infrequently to the detriment of the impasto of the pigments.

The removal of the old layer of varnish, be it by the dry method through rubbing with the hand, or by means of spirits, is not always effected with the necessary circumspection. Something of the original colour can easily be attacked. If the original layer of colour is grainy and rough, the darkened varnish has settled in the depths and can hardly be rubbed off without injury to the original paint. Incidentally in many cases the endeavour to remove the old varnish radically, down to the last vestige, appears by no means so desirable as to justify running the risk which I have indicated.

We can remember many sensational incidents over which the newspapers busied themselves. A restorer had put right a picture—that is he had removed the old varnish and perhaps also some repaint. At once accusations were heard that he had 'overcleaned' the picture, rubbed down its genuine glazes and reduced its artistic value. Such an indignation—usually expressed by people who never had paid any attention to the picture before it was 'damaged'—is mostly unjustified, if only for the reason that the picture may have been overcleaned already before it was last cleaned, and that, strictly speaking, only someone

37. NARRATIVE SUBJECT

Forgery dating from the middle of the 19th century, in subject and costume full of childish impossibilities. There exist many forgeries produced by the same workshop

who was present at the restoration ought to have a right to judge. Moreover the hard, cool, and naked appearance shown by the picture immediately after being cleaned proves in itself nothing against the restorer. Our taste depends on convention. We are not accustomed to perceive the original condition, more particularly so, for example, in a Gallery like the Louvre, where almost every picture, under many layers of dull varnish, disproportionately warm and dark, shows the cheapest form of harmony. A cleaned picture, among such as are not cleaned, looks over-cleaned. Our eyes are enervated and spoiled. The aspect worn by the pictures, when they originally left the workshops, would shock us as being crude and motley. The earlier restorers knew this well and, after cleaning the pictures, used to make them 'old' —that is warm and 'harmonious'—once more, by means of coloured varnish. A continuous change in the demands, in the prejudices, is to be expected. Especially in German museums one has got accustomed to the appearance of cleaned, and occasionally over-cleaned, pictures.

The activity of the restorer becomes highly problematical the moment there presents itself the question of making up for deficiencies—that is, of filling gaps or revivifying passages which have been rubbed. Here the various wishes, demands and aims part company. The historian, to whom the work of art is a record, opposes, from his standpoint, with full justification, that kind of restoration which goes beyond preserving and exposing. He demands to see clearly what is left of the original, but wishes it also not to be concealed from him that something of the original is missing. It is precisely the successful re-integration that is distasteful to him: the unsuccessful one he, of course, detects easily and can make allowance for. The picture-owners, in whose service and in conformity with whose wishes the restorer works—collectors or dealers—take up a different standpoint from that of the scholar. What they demand is not so much the document which has been cleaned and gives reliable information as, rather, the maximum of value—and, indeed, not only artistic value but also market value. Every damage, as long as it remains visible, lowers the market value. The restorer must conceal such damage. The serious lover of art and the museum official, who supervises and directs the work of the restorer, are inclined to side with the scholar. And, as a matter of fact, the purist faction has lately gained adherents. Now and then you find in public galleries carefully cleaned pictures whose defective portions have been left open—say, have been filled in with a neutral tint. There is this to be submitted in favour of such a procedure, that the best restorer is ineffectual when it is a question of filling gaps, especially if it is a question of parts which are of fundamental importance for the total impression of the picture.

The decision—apparently unavoidable—against

38. BRUGES MASTER, MADONNA WITH TWO FEMALE SAINTS

Formerly London Art Market

Much rubbed, painted about 1480

every re-integrating restoration is, however, beset with practical difficulties. If part of the original pigments are missing in a panel of the 14th century, it is still possible to derive some enjoyment from what is left, and in one's imagination to fill the gaps which have remained open. The position changes, however, if gaps are visible in the midst of a picture of the 17th century. They do away with the illusion of a spatial whole, and destroy the effect. In every case it must be carefully considered whether a more or less questionable addition, made by a restorer, is not to be regarded as the lesser evil; just as a surgeon always should ask himself whether the success to be expected from an operation is so great and so certain that it outweighs the danger entailed by the operation. It is, no doubt, possible to choose a middle course, namely, to fill in the hole in such a fashion that the defective passage does not strike the eye as something that disturbs the general effect, but yet becomes obvious if you look closely. Such a procedure has the defect of all half-measures.

As long as works of art in private ownership are regarded as representing financial values, so long will the restorer again and again find himself forced into the part of the forger.

There exist underground connections between the workshops of the restorers and of the forgers. Years ago I saw in the possession of a London dealer a pretty Bruges picture of about 1480 which was greatly rubbed, a full-length figure of the Madonna with two female saints. A Belgian restorer then got hold of it. I do not know whether he restored it: in any case I have not seen it again. But a forgery, based on it, did turn up, considerably larger and more imposing than the archetype. A small misfortune had, incidentally, befallen the forger. St. Catherine, receiving the ring from the Infant Christ, was depicted; the ring was, however, no longer recognizable in the poorly preserved original. In the copy, the Infant Christ busies himself quite unaccountably with the finger of the saint, since He has no ring to bestow.

39. MADONNA WITH TWO FEMALE SAINTS
Forgery based on the picture by the Bruges Master, Plate 38

XXXVIII

ON ART LITERATURE

LANGUAGE is poor and inadequate, but it is nevertheless the only vehicle at our disposal; an obtuse instrument which we must untiringly try to perfect. At the same time we should bear in mind that sharp knives easily become blunt. Emotions resemble butterflies: speared by the needle of the word, they lose their life. All that is said on art sounds like a poor translation.

The arts have a common root, are interconnected in the depths: poetry, music and the arts of the eye. Whoever is bound to convey by word the impression of a picture or a piece of sculpture, finds himself impelled towards poetical expression, while his intelligence cautions him to avoid poetry. Not wholly unjustifiably it has been said by somebody that one ought to be musical in order fully to understand formative art. There is some truth in this sweeping maxim inasmuch as music, in preference to all other arts, is absolute art, and hence can put us on the

s

273

direct road to that which has the characteristics of specific art.

If one enquires into art literature—which has assumed such gigantic proportions—with reference to substance, fertility and permanent value, one will find that there remains little enough, nothing more than the translation into speech of visual impressions. Most certainly the word can never replace the optical experience, but he who has some command of language may well be able to help the man who hears better than he sees, to 'understand' the work of art —as the inappropriately rationalistic expression goes.

The higher the artistic value, the deeper the impression, the farther does description depart from sober and matter-of-fact chronicling, in order to approach poetic re-creation, which, it is true, must be checked with circumspection if it is not to degenerate into obscurity and empty word-play. You cannot, let us say, by means of words produce so graphic an impression of the type of woman of Hugo van der Goes that a work by this master might be recognized as such from that account; but the description can definitely, as a guiding interpretation, deepen the impression and increase the capacity for recognition in anybody who has the work before him. And in so doing it performs at any rate something. We say, for instance, 'the lean, stark, pale, bony forms have been moulded from within by profound and sublime thought, by emotional distress and struggle'. It is possible for an imitative artist to reproduce a picture thus described, but, since he lacks the inspiring force, he is unlikely to get beyond empty masks and caricatures, sorrowful expressions bereft of cause, and seriousness with no foundation.

The more deeply observation and notation have penetrated into spiritually emotional existence, the better will the reader—who, however, must not only be a reader—be enabled to carry out an investigation based on criticism of style, and especially to unmask copies and forgeries.

There do not exist many authors whose literary capacity is on a level with their understanding of art. Among the living men in Germany the one whose performance, in interpreting by language visual experiences, stands out, is perhaps—alongside Heinrich Wölfflin—Wilhelm Fraenger.

The ideal of the art scholar, expressing himself by means of language, was perhaps realized in Carl Justi. In him extensive knowledge of historical facts united itself with the capacity to experience the process of artistic activity. I refer the reader to his book on Velazquez. From the impression which the work of art has produced on him, he immediately conjures up the situation in which the master found himself; that which was demanded of him, that which he wanted. He provides psychological interpretations of the visible from knowledge of historical circumstances.

The re-creation of the work of art, in which but few

have succeeded, is something very different from the itemized description which the writers of catalogues provide with more or less ability. It has partly become superfluous, alongside of the photographic reproduction, and is largely ineffectual, since the unfortunate reader is hardly capable of constructing a connected idea of the whole from a large number of data. The enumeration of colour values, which in many catalogues of recent date is meant to supplement the black-and-white illustrations, demands from memory the impossible. The courageous and interesting attempt—made in the catalogue of the Donaueschingen Gallery, published in 1921—in which the colours are itemized with letters and figures in conformity with Ostwald's plates, has remained a curiosity.

So far as I can see, the endeavour to overcome the barren pedantry of the customary catalogue description has been successful but once, namely, in Rudolf Eigenberger's volume on the Gallery of the Vienna Academy. Here the mirror of words has, successfully and in an exemplary fashion, caught the total effect, the artistic significance of each picture; and the individual data regarding form and colour are not just set out one after the other, but on the contrary dovetailed into a connected whole.

A double request is addressed to description and cataloguing. For one thing we want to have the subject explained, to be enlightened about iconography, and to have laid down for us what the master had to do,

40. REMBRANDT
MOSES SHOWING THE TABLES OF THE LAW TO THE PEOPLE
not 'Moses breaking the Tables of the Law'
Berlin, Picture Gallery
1659

and what he intended. Secondly, we want a description of that which is visible, a translation of the impression received, and a statement of what the master has done. Analysing erudition is to be avoided in performing the second task: the impression must be received at first hand and with our senses fully receptive; and it is to be canalized into the form provided by language, without prejudice, and without reliance on thought.

An instructive illustration of the interconnection between iconographical learning and naïve directness in the contemplation of a picture was not long ago provided by an article by Dr. Heppner.[1] Fault has often been found with a picture by Rembrandt in the Berlin Gallery which, as was thought and may be read everywhere, represents Moses, who, in his anger, breaks the tables of the Law. The impression produced by the movement and the face of the hero did not fulfil the expectations raised by the subject. Dr. Heppner has now proved that Rembrandt in reality was faced with quite a different subject—the law-giver who *shows* the tables to the people. We now no longer miss the explosion of anger, the powerful action; on the contrary, from our better knowledge, we can appreciate the dignified exaltation of the figure. We learn, too, that the picture is but a fragment; we can supply from our imagination that which is missing, and our impression and judgment change.

[1] See Heppner in *Oud Holland*, 1935, p. 241.

ON ART LITERATURE

A disadvantage of the terminology of art history consists in this, that aesthetic concepts are not sufficiently clearly differentiated from such as relate to time. In art literature of the 19th century, certain art forms of the 17th century were censured by applying to them the expression 'Baroque', and this term was retained for those forms at a time when they had become admired and appreciated. At present the word 'Baroque' is used, now in a sense aesthetically derogatory, now in order to convey the neutral notion of date, and confusion follows. Similar remarks apply to the concept 'Romantic'. One should never use these terms without defining them clearly.

To every description which aims at conveying a sense of character, there attaches something of the caricature, since the web, which means the totality of qualities, is destroyed if you pick out a thread in order to show it for the purpose of emphasis. You need not, however, fight shy of such distortion, as long as you remain conscious of the one-sidedness, and ready to neutralize it by other utterances. The contradictions which ensue, and which belong to the nature of all psychological knowledge, are not to be feared. Just as man is full of contradictions, so is everything that he does or creates.

Descriptions or statements, elaborate and aiming at completeness, demand too much of the visual memory of the reader; it is the aphorisms, throwing light like flashes, which are above all effective. The last sentence contains perhaps less of a truth that is universally valid than a contention *pro domo*, by means of which reasons are given for a personal peculiarity or, maybe, an apology is offered for a personal weakness.

INDEX

INDEX

282

INDEX

283

INDEX